Consequences
Morality, Ethics, and the Future

James H. Burtness

Fortress Press
Minneapolis

CONSEQUENCES
Morality, Ethics, and the Future

Scripture quotations from the New Revised Standard Version of the Bible are copyright © 1989 by the Division of Christian Education of the National Council of Churches of Christ in the United States of America and are used by permission.

Cover design: Michael Mihelich
Interior design: Beth Wright

Material used in Chapter 4 from *Philosophical Ethics: An Introduction to Moral Philosophy*, 2d ed., by Tom Beauchamp, is copyright © 1991 McGraw-Hill Companies and is used by permission. Material on page 71 from *A Farewell to Arms* by Ernest Hemingway is copyright © 1929 Charles Scribner's Sons, renewed © 1957 Ernest Hemingway and © Hemingway Foreign Rights Trust, and is used by permission of Scribner, a Division of Simon & Schuster, Inc., and Hemingway Foreign Rights Trust.

Library of Congress Cataloging-in-Publication Data

Burtness, James H.
    Consequences: morality, ethics, and the future / James H. Burtness.
        p.   cm.
    Includes bibliographical references.
    ISBN 0-8006-3092-0 (pbk. : alk. paper)
    1. Christian ethics.   I. Title.
BJ1251.B87   1999
241—dc21   99-17002
                                                       CIP

The paper used in this publication meets the minimum requirements of American National Standard for Information Sciences—Permanence of Paper for Printed Library Materials, ANSI Z329.48-1984.

Manufactured in the U.S.A.   AF 1-3092
03   02   01   00   99   1   2   3   4   5   6   7   8   9   10

For Matthew, Alex, Bert, Anna, Anton, Laura, and Lily
—*each one an ode to joy*

Contents

Preface ⟿

This is a book about Christian Ethics. It is a book, however, that acknowledges that not only Christians do ethics, and that not only Christians lead moral lives. It acknowledges that some who are not Christians may lead more exemplary lives than some who are, and that Christians may have much to learn about ethical reflection from some people who think clearly and speak helpfully about morality but who do not share Christian faith commitments. This does not mean that opinions about the distinctiveness, or even possibly the uniqueness, of Christian Ethics are summarily dismissed. In fact, readers will find that Christian claims about God and the whole created order, together with implications of these claims for the moral life, are integral to the main argument of this book. The point is that Christian Ethics as a field of enquiry requires that attention be paid both to possible disjunctions and to possible connections between faith and life, or confession and conduct, or believing and behaving. The Foreword and the Afterword are thus designed as bookends to be kept in mind throughout the reading of the rest of the text.

The reader will not find here pieces of moral admonition and counsel. This is not a handbook that claims to lead the reader to the making of right moral decisions. It is not a list of moral issues with the opinion of the author on each item, nor a catalog of case studies designed to stimulate moral debate, nor a declaration about what is wrong in the world and what must be done to make things right. Materials dealing with such things are readily available and can be very useful.

This book is an attempt to step back from such urgent matters, to find some perspective from which to look carefully at them, to reflect on options for thinking about them, and to assist in the formulating of ways to talk about them constructively. A specific goal is to help people with serious moral disagreements to come into civil and productive conversation with one another. Clear distinctions are thus made in the first two sections between the institution of morality as having to do with human behavior, and the discipline of ethics as

having to do with reflecting on and engaging in constructive conversation about that behavior. These distinctions are of great importance.
Thus "morality" and "ethics" appear as separate terms in the subtitle
of the book and have separate sections of the book devoted to them.

This work is primarily an attempt to describe, rather than to persuade. The goal is not that readers will come to agree with the
author, but that readers will come to agree with themselves. That is,
it is hoped that readers will gain greater awareness of how they actually make moral decisions, draw implications from their basic moral
commitments, reach conclusions about matters that they consider to
be moral, and think about the fundamental nature of morality itself.

Gaining greater insight into how one actually functions morally
and bringing one's action and reflection into some kind of congruence do not mean that struggle and uncertainty will disappear. One
may, indeed, become more tentative in one's judgments. Yet such
insight ought to give a person some degree of confidence in moral
matters and ought to equip one better to enter into helpful conversation with those with whom one has serious and difficult disagreements. The assumption here is that it is usually, not necessarily
always, better to think clearly about one's actions than to be naive
about them, and usually better to converse calmly about moral disagreements than to shout defiantly about them.

There is also a point of view presented and argued here, even
though the book attempts to be primarily descriptive rather than
persuasive. The position is specific in the title of this book, and it is
detailed in the third section. Alert readers will not be surprised to
discover that a consequentialist position begins to evidence itself
even in the first two sections. Necessary decisions about how to present materials make totally objective description impossible. Nevertheless, a serious attempt has been made to be both fair and accurate
throughout the text. The hope is that engagement with commitments of the author will help readers to engage more constructively
with commitments of their own.

The entire rationale for the discipline of ethics—the commitment
to the importance of carefully organizing ways to think about morality and reach conclusions about what one considers to be moral matters—may be quite new and somewhat strange to some readers.
What is morally right and wrong may seem so obvious and immediate to some that stopping to think about it may even be regarded as

an excuse to delay the doing of what one already knows to be the right thing to do. The entire premise of this book may strike some as not only odd or excessively complicated, but in fact deleterious rather than beneficial to moral life. The hope is that such readers might find the description of a position other than their own to be at least interesting and perhaps even stimulating.

To get some feel for what is being attempted in this text, whether or not one finally finds things with which to agree, it could be useful to read through the thesis statements for each chapter. After getting a sense of the movement of the whole, one ought to be able to know where one is at any point along the way as the presentation unfolds.

There are sufficient references to other literature so that those who wish will be able to pursue a particular point in more detail, or to identify materials for further reading. But no attempt at exhaustive documentation has been made. The author acknowledges indebtedness to a great many laborers in the field of ethics, as well as to colleagues, students, and other treasured friends who have been significant conversation partners along the way.

Among these there is one who demonstrates a continuing and pervasive interest in my work, one who is always eager for serious and detailed debate about matters of importance. Her name is Dolores, and she has been my partner in all things now for more than four decades. My 1985 book, *Shaping the Future: The Ethics of Dietrich Bonhoeffer,* was dedicated to her. An earlier exploration in ethics (1967), *Whatever You Do: An Essay in Christian Ethics,* was dedicated to our four children. This book is dedicated to our grandchildren, who will face moral quandaries more complex and more difficult than those faced by their grandparents and parents. Our prayer is that they will be persons of robust faith and that they will lead useful lives. It is also that they will know why they believe and behave as they do, and that they will be well equipped to converse calmly and wisely about their lives with contemporaries whose behaviors, for good or ill, may be accompanied by very different commitments.

A final word of gratitude goes to Eric Berg, my current teaching assistant, for his cheerful and competent response to a wide variety of requests. He has been a gift.

Luther Seminary
St. Paul, Minnesota

Foreword

Moral Behavior and Christian Faith: Disjunctions

1. Behaving and Believing

And they'll know we are Christians by our love, by our love.
Yes, they'll know we are Christians by our love.
                                                    —*Peter Scholtes*

It is essential to distinguish moral behavior from Christian faith. Moral behavior does not constitute Christian faith, and Christian faith does not assure moral behavior.

Christians have for decades enjoyed singing, "And they'll know we are Christians by our love, by our love." It sounds good and may even inspire some Christians to live in a more loving way. But it is difficult to imagine any thoughtful Christian thinking that these lyrics actually state the fact of the matter. People apparently did look at the early Christians and say, "Look how they love one another."[1] Certainly there are many Christians who are very loving people. But it should be obvious that there are many people who behave in a loving way and reject as false what Christians believe to be true, and also that there are many Christian believers who fail, some of them frequently, to behave in ways that others regard as loving. Nobody would be interested in singing it, but if the lyrics were to be changed into a more accurate statement, they might read something like this: "They will know by our loving behavior that we are probably loving people. But they will know from that fact alone absolutely nothing about what we believe concerning God and the creation, or about who we believe Jesus Christ to be."

This is a book about "Christian Ethics." The term is used to refer to a great variety of attempts to present materials having to do with behaving and believing, or more specifically with moral behaving and Christian believing and what these two might have to do with one another.

There are Christian Ethics works that deal with the history, or a particular segment of the history, of Christian behaving and believing. Some works concentrate on biblical materials or particular biblical documents or authors. There are multitudes of works dealing with, for example, the ethics of Jesus, the ethics of Paul, the Sermon on the Mount, or the message of the Hebrew prophets. Many works in Christian Ethics could be called "practical" works, in that they seek to be immediately useful to Christian believers seeking guidance about what behaviors, in the opinion of the author, follow or ought to follow from Christian faith.

This book pays attention to historical and biblical materials and seeks in the end to be useful, but it is primarily a constructive effort. An attempt is made here to put together important ways of thinking about behaving and believing that will provide the reader with necessary tools for working at the intersection of these two activities. In the Afterword some possible connections will be suggested. In this Foreword the point is to suggest the significance of disjunctions. Behaving and believing must be clearly distinguished.

To say that these two must be distinguished is not to say that they should be separated. Jesus had harsh things to say about those who said, "Lord, Lord," but did not do the will of God (Matt. 7:21). John questioned how the love of God can abide in those who have the world's goods and yet refuse to help those in need (1 John 3:17). Martin Luther said that faith is a living, busy, active, mighty thing, and that it is active, specifically, in love for the neighbor.[2] Dietrich Bonhoeffer coined the term "cheap grace" for the notion that the reception of God's grace carries with it no obligations for serious discipleship.

> Cheap grace is the preaching of forgiveness without requiring repentance, baptism without Church discipline, Communion without confession, absolution without contrition. Cheap grace is grace without discipleship, grace without the Cross, grace without Jesus Christ, living and incarnate.[3]

Few are impressed by speech unaccompanied by action. Those who talk the talk are expected also to walk the walk.

Behaving and believing must not be separated, but the two are not identical or interchangeable. If any clarity about Christian Ethics is going to be achieved, it is essential to distinguish them from one another. It is not possible to determine with any accuracy what a person believes from knowledge about how that person behaves, and it is not possible to determine with any accuracy how a person will behave from knowledge about what that person believes.

The first assertion is that how a person behaves does not provide immediate and accurate information about what that person believes. This distinction is built into most carefully developed legal systems. There may be no question about whether a person has committed a murder. It may have been clearly and voluntarily confessed, and the evidence may be incontrovertible. Yet the court must make a judgment about intent, about what was in the mind of the murderer before, during, and after the murder. The court will usually deal more strenuously with premeditated murder than with what it judges to be a crime of passion. But the judgment is often complex and difficult. There is no quick or easy way to move from how a person behaves to a judgment about what that person believes to be the case at the time of the deed. There is an important and necessary distinction, a certain distance, between behaving and believing.

In *Fiddler on the Roof*,[4] Tevye asks his wife Golde, "Do you love me?" She replies, "For twenty-five years I washed your clothes. . . ." We all recognize the poignancy of the conversation that follows. Loving a person may well have something to do with clothes washing. But there is no automatic guarantee that washing clothes grows out of love, nor that love will result in clothes washing. The love question cannot be resolved so simply. Near the end of the conversation, the complexity is agonizingly expressed in Golde's answer, "I suppose I do." The internal commitments of a person cannot be quickly or unequivocally correlated with external actions. As the thesis statement of this chapter states, moral behavior does not constitute Christian faith.

One problem that arises from failing to make this distinction is that Christians may find themselves identifying others as Christians, even though these people explicitly state that they are not Christians. The mistake comes from thinking that anyone who behaves like a Christian must also believe as a Christian believes. Sometimes the word "really" is added. "This person is really a Christian, even though she won't admit it." Sometimes the word "anonymous" is used.[5] Someone may say, "Gandhi was an 'anonymous' Christian because he behaved like a Christian even though he rejected Christian faith commitments about Jesus Christ." Or the word "unconscious" may be used. Bonhoeffer writes, "The question how there can be a 'natural piety' is at the same time the question of 'unconscious Christianity,' with which I'm more and more concerned."[6] Someone may say, "He is an 'unconscious' Christian." Some who consider themselves "conscious" Christians think that in this case the problem is simply to bring what is "unconscious" to the level of consciousness.

There may be some truth tucked away in some of these comments, when used in properly qualified ways about certain individuals. Such designations are most often used by Christians who mean well and wish to be "inclusive," to embrace into their own fold people who behave the way they think Christians should behave. It is often, quite to the contrary, an arrogant and morally imperialistic attack on people who know they are not Christians, state that fact explicitly, and rightly resent the notion that only Christian believers can behave in exemplary ways.

The second half of the thesis assertion of this chapter is that Christian faith does not assure moral behavior. It is perhaps more obvious and more widely acknowledged than the first half. All serious Christians know that they stray, at least occasionally, from whatever it is they consider the moral path to be. This straying may be attributed to common human frailty: "To err is human." It may, in a more sophisticated way, be linked to the Christian confession that we are creatures, not the Creator, and thus severely limited in our capacity to live in the loving way that God lives. More specifically, the disjunctions between believing and behaving are taken to be the result of what Christians call "sin," a deep and pervasive moral sickness that penetrates the character and the conduct of all human beings in relation to both God and neighbor.

The Bible is full of reminders of this fact. "All we like sheep have gone astray; we have all turned to our own way" (Isa. 53:6). "There is no one who is righteous, not even one" (Rom. 3:10). "Therefore, just as sin came into the world through one man, and death came through sin, and so death spread to all because all have sinned" (Rom. 5:12). The confession of sin is in some central location in all expressions of Christian believing, and in the liturgical traditions it is carefully built into the pattern of worship prior to the announcement of the absolution, the forgiveness of sin. Even those Christian groups that entertain some notion of "Christian perfection" treat this as a theoretical, or more properly a theological, possibility rather than as a common actuality. It is well established in the Bible and in Christian history and theology that Christian faith does not assure moral behavior.

A problem that arises from the failure to distinguish behaving and believing in this second way is that one Christian may decide that another, who confesses Christian faith and believes that Christian claims are true, may be judged to be not a Christian because that person's behavior does not seem to meet expected moral standards. Again, the word "really" may be added. "She says she is a Christian, but she really is not. If she were, she would not behave the way she does." The mistake of confusing behaving and believing has in this case subtly but surely resulted in elevating behaving, rather than believing, into the role of chief criterion for determining who may legitimately be called a Christian.

Something that too often arises from the false notion that Christian faith assures moral behavior is that elected and appointed church officials tend to regard their own moral judgments as the only legitimate conclusions to which Christians can come on serious and often enormously complex issues. Loyal members of Christian congregations can be thankful that it is not universal among church leaders. But it is painfully prevalent. There are important structural and procedural differences, significant theological and political variations among such diverse groups as Roman Catholics, Assemblies of God, Baptists, Lutherans, Methodists. In every Christian group, however, there is unfortunately a tendency among leaders not only to think that Christian faith assures moral behavior, but that knowledge of the details of this moral behavior is somehow granted to them more directly and more clearly than it is to those whom they are selected to serve, to energize, to "lead."

What sometimes results is a tendency to think that the proclamation of the Good News about Jesus that leads to believing will take care of itself, and that the important thing is to instruct "lay people" in the "Christian answers" to complex economic, political, and social problems and even to the proper solution to intricate global tensions. Christians sitting in the pew, reading church publications, or following in the media the political pronouncements and activities of their church bodies and selected leaders can, when they find themselves in disagreement, only suffer in silence or work at the very difficult task of dissent. When the essential distinction between behaving and believing is neglected, dissent with those in power becomes at the least a heroic enterprise. Christian faith does not assure moral behavior. Certainly it does not assure that moral judgments of church leaders are automatically more valid than moral judgments made by those Christians not designated as leaders.

What happens then, too often, is that the careful and calm ethical reflection that should take place among Christians concerning important moral disagreements fails to materialize. Instead of affirming that there is one Lord, one faith, one baptism, and then moving to serious exploration about what implications for judgments concerning moral matters can legitimately be entertained, leaders are too often inclined to think their job is to teach others to come into agreement with their own judgments. Instead of serious conversation, what results is political power plays that make secular governmental procedures look uncommonly civilized.

The failure to distinguish carefully between behaving and believing can have serious consequences. Some of these have been suggested. Another way to state the problem is that the discipline of ethics cannot begin until the legitimacy of differing moral judgments is acknowledged. If a person thinks that only her own moral judgments are correct, there is no room for true conversation. If a Christian thinks that his own moral judgments are not judgments at all, but in fact the only true correlation between moral behavior and Christian faith, believing is inevitably replaced by behaving as the criterion for Christian identity.

If the discipline of Christian Ethics is going to go anywhere, to be worth anything, even to get underway, it is essential for Christians to identify themselves primarily in terms of believing rather than in terms of behaving. Some may think this deprecates moral behavior. The argument here is that it does the exact opposite. It makes serious conversation about moral disagreements possible by locating moral behavior in its proper place, which, wherever that location, is not identical to the location of Christian faith.

The Apostles' Creed says a great deal about what Christians believe, not a single word about how Christians behave or ought to behave. The ancient Christian distinction between behaving and believing is observed in the ecumenical creeds, liturgical rites, and worship practices of wide varieties of Christians throughout the ages.

There are important disjunctions between behaving and believing, specifically between moral behavior and Christian faith. One way to look at this is to say that moral behavior does not constitute Christian faith, and that Christian faith does not assure moral behavior. Another way to look at this disjunction is to ask about possible relationships concerning morality, humanity, and Christianity.

Matt 17 Chapter - why do you Call me Lord when you don't do what I say?

Foreword —

2. Morality, Humanity, and Christianity

At the beginning of the new millennium, Christians make up about one-third of the global population.
— *1995 Encyclopedia Britannica Book of the Year*

Morality is an interest common to all human beings, even though understandings of morality vary widely. Understandings of Christianity vary widely, but interest in Christianity is not common to all human beings.

Another way to talk about disjunctions between moral behavior and Christian faith is to say that morality is of interest to a great many more people than is Christianity. This is important, because Christians need to be aware when they talk about morality that they are discussing something in which people who are not Christians have interests, opinions, passions, knowledge, experience, expertise. Christians need to know that they share their interest in morality with everyone else. They may respond to this fact in various ways, but to ignore it is to run the risk of being ruled out of conversations that may be of critical importance not only for Christians, but for all human beings.

This is not to say that morality is more important than faith. For the author faith is, finally, more important than morality. It is not to say that Christians should regard Christian faith as one religion among many, all of which should mute their faith differences in order to work together to improve the moral climate among world populations. The author believes, on the contrary, that Christianity is a missionary faith that believes its claims to be true. Certainly, among those claims is confidence that there can be moral benefits connected with Christian faith. It seems difficult to imagine, in fact, that any thinking person would remain a Christian if that person were convinced that the consequences of Christian faith and life through the centuries have been primarily deleterious, rather than beneficial, for humankind and the rest of creation.

When Christians deal with morality, they have no right to expect an automatic hearing. If someone who is not a Christian considers interesting something that Christians say about morality, it will not be because the speakers are Christians, but because they have something interesting to say.

The assertion that morality is an interest common to all human beings is not a claim that every human being is equally interested in morality. If one were to devise an instrument to determine degrees of interest in morality, it would likely show that the great majority of people are somewhere in the middle of a bell curve. There is pervasive interest in morality, even though at the edges of the curve interests may thin out. Complicating the issue, as has been suggested, is the variety of notions about what the word "morality" means.

Such an instrument would probably show that there are those at the extreme ends of the curve who relate to moral matters in almost opposite ways. There are individuals who are so limited in intellectual or emotional capacity, or who have been so deprived or abused in the period when they should have been nurtured, that their sensitivity to and interest in morality may be negligible. A "cold-blooded killer" apparently murders with no feeling whatsoever for the victim. A "pathological liar" may be able to tell lies with such serenity that a polygraph test administered by an expert may fail to register a problem. There may be individuals with almost no interest in morality. On the other hand, there are people whose behavior is hindered by excessive moral scrupulosity, people so paralyzed by the thought that they may do something wrong that they sit on their hands and fail to do anything at all. Degrees of moral sensitivity and interest do exist.

The variety of views on morality has to do not only with positions on moral issues or with conclusions reached when considering moral cases, but also with what issues should be considered to be moral issues and what cases should be addressed as moral cases. When one person says to another, "Well, now, that's a moral issue!" the other may reply, "It is not a moral issue at all. It is a matter of lifestyle." Or it may be argued that instead of being a moral issue, it is a matter of legality, culture and custom, age, or gender. There are varieties of

ways in which the word "morality" is used, and there is no simple
way to settle disputes about uses of the term. Jeffrey Stout argues
persuasively in his *Ethics after Babel* that we are currently in a tower
of Babel in our attempts at ethical discourse because we do not even
have a common understanding of the meaning of words fundamental to the conversation.[1] Morality is understood in a wide variety of
ways, but that does not diminish the fact that morality is a common
human interest.

The other side of this coin, that not all human beings are interested in Christianity, should be obvious. The Christian gospel is
intended for all; Jesus sent his followers to make disciples of all peoples. Those who believe that the Christian claim is not just useful but
true also believe that every human being is a person capable of coming to this realization. There is a universal intent about the Christian
proclamation, yet interest in that proclamation is not universal.

To say that not everyone is interested in Christianity is different
from any assertion about human interest in religion. If religion were
the issue and this book were about "religious ethics," other factors
would come into play. For example, some wish to argue that every
human being has a deep religious center, a yearning for God, an
awareness of the transcendent. Augustine said, " . . . you made us for
yourself and our hearts find no peace until they rest in you."[2]
Friedrich Schleiermacher thought that the consciousness of our
absolute dependence, our feeling of dependence on God, was the
common element in all religious faiths.[3] Paul Tillich called it "ultimate concern."[4] John Cobb has worked with the notion of that
which is supremely important.[5] Alcoholics Anonymous has built
into its twelve-step program a step that acknowledges a "Power
greater than ourselves"—an acknowledgment considered possible
and necessary for everyone involved in recovery from addictions.
This claim about the incurably religious nature of human beings
may or may not be true. It does not in any case affect the fact that not
all human beings are interested in Christianity. No matter how
widely one allows varieties of understanding Christianity to go,
Christianity cannot be equated with either religion or morality. It
interests fewer people than either.

Any serious treatment of Christian Ethics must deal with this
fact, that morality is of interest to many more people than is Chris-

tianity, because Christians need to be able to talk calmly and con-structively about moral matters with people who do not share their faith commitments. One way to deal with it would be to begin with what one considers to be a Christian perspective on morality, and then to argue that this perspective ought to be of some interest to everyone. In this book, the opposite route is taken. An attempt will be made to discuss morality as a common human phenomenon, and then to look at various models of ethical reflection on that phenom-enon. In the third section Christian claims will be brought to bear on the construction of a specific proposal for doing ethics in Christian perspective. The move is from disjunctions between moral behavior and Christian faith toward connections. When disjunctions are being considered, even the combining of the two terms "Christian" and "Ethics" raises important questions.

Foreword ⟶

3. Questions about "Christian Ethics"

Is there such a thing as a Christian ethic?
— *Dietrich Bonhoeffer*

Christians have commitments to both moral behavior and Christian faith. The combining of these two in the single term "Christian Ethics" raises serious questions.

⟶ ⟶

This is a book about Christian Ethics. It is important to begin by noting that there are significant disjunctions between behaving and believing, and that a great many more people demonstrate an interest in morality than in Christianity. Adding to the difficulty is the fact that even the term "Christian Ethics" is problematic.

Does "Christian" qualify the word "ethics" slightly or radically? That is, is *Christian* ethics essentially similar to or essentially different from ethics done without that qualification? On the one hand, it is possible to emphasize similarities. Christians, as well as others, should tell the truth and keep promises, should stop at the red light and proceed on the green, should be kind to others. Ethical reflection on such moral matters is viewed by some as a common human enterprise with little, if any, specifically Christian content. On the other hand, it is possible to emphasize the distinctiveness of Christian faith and its implications for behavior. It can be argued that Christians are held to not only a higher standard, but one that is essentially different. It may be said that "sacrificial love" may not only go beyond "common morality," but that it constitutes a different criterion altogether. Few Christians, for example, would expect the call to take up one's cross and follow Jesus to make any sense to people with no interest in Christianity.

Whether one holds that Christian Ethics is essentially similar to or essentially different from other ethics, questions still remain about why one thinks as one does, and what implications of one's way of thinking might be both for moral behavior and for Christian faith. There are many who have struggled with questions that arise when the term "Christian Ethics" is used.

Dietrich Bonhoeffer struggled with what the term might mean. When teaching at the University of Berlin, he gave a lecture on the subject "Is There Such a Thing as a Christian Ethic?"[1] It is a finely textured discussion, but the main point Bonhoeffer makes is that there is no such thing as Christian behavior that can be so closely tied to Christian faith that one becomes an equivalent that can be substituted for the other. Nothing, not even exemplary moral behavior, should be allowed to obscure the fact that the primary focus of Christianity is on the person and work of Jesus Christ, rather than on the moral behavior of Christian people. Bonhoeffer worries that if acts or patterns of moral behavior, or specific ways to do ethical reflection on that behavior, are labeled "Christian," serious problems arise. One is that people who behave according to the pattern may be labeled "Christian" against their will. Another is that appropriate allowances for differences in moral judgment among Christians may be stifled. Bonhoeffer worked on these themes throughout his life and detailed his mature reflections in the book titled *Ethics,* compiled and edited by Eberhard Bethge after Bonhoeffer's death.[2]

The same concern was central in the work of Karl Barth. Although editors have published posthumously some of his work under the title *Ethics,* Barth insisted during his lifetime that there is something intrinsically inappropriate in any attempt to talk about Christian life apart from very specific talk about Christian faith. He was therefore reluctant to publish works entitled "Christian Ethics." That did not mean that he had no interest in the Christian life. It meant, rather, that he wanted to be clear that Christian life flows from Christian faith. Life cannot be equated to faith. It cannot be substituted for faith. Christian life can have no freestanding existence apart from Christian faith. In *Church Dogmatics,* Barth makes this point dramatically by finishing each volume with a section on ethical implications of the doctrine being handled.

Barth's point is the same as Bonhoeffer's. Christianity has to do with a faith response to the person and work of Jesus Christ. There are implications of this for moral behavior and ethical reflection, but Christianity cannot be described purely in terms of this behavior or reflection. There can be no such thing as Christian Ethics apart from Christian proclamation and confession. According to Bonhoeffer and Barth, it is essential that Christians be more certain and more committed to Christian faith than they are to what they consider to be the implications of this faith for morality and ethics. This does not lead to a casual attitude toward the behavior of Christians. Bonhoeffer went to his death because he was convinced that he must act on his convictions about the implications of Christian faith for moral behavior, in his case resulting in active resistance to Adolf Hitler. But he never confused morality with faith, even in the final days prior to his execution by the Nazis.

Another person who has struggled with this question, but in ways different from Bonhoeffer and Barth, is James Gustafson. He speaks to it directly in a book entitled *Can Ethics Be Christian?*[3] Anyone who thinks that the only answer to that question is "Of course!" will find that answer seriously questioned in Gustafson's engaging discussion. In another volume, *Christ and the Moral Life,* he struggles with the question again, but in a different way.[4] He formulates his task in this case by asking about those differences for the moral life that commitment to Jesus Christ can, ought to, and often does make. All three verb forms are necessary in order to get at the many dimensions of the question. He organizes his responses to the question in five very helpful groupings of material. In his major constructive work, Gustafson still writes as a Christian doing ethics but frames the question in yet another way. He writes about *Ethics from a Theocentric Perspective,*[5] indicating that the major focus of ethical reflection for a Christian ought to be the relation between God and the creation, rather than between Jesus Christ and those who confess his name and seek to follow him. In this work, Gustafson questions the term "Christian Ethics" by saying that Christians are people who know that their behavior should be thought about in relation to God and God's creation, that is, in theocentric rather than in anthropocentric or strictly Christocentric perspective.

Paul Ramsey, one of the most careful and articulate Christian ethicists of the mid-twentieth century, always worked in close touch with the Bible and with the Christian tradition. He said that he always did ethics as the Christian ethicist he was. Yet on the basis of specifically Christian sources, he affirmed universal moral imperatives—obligations applicable to all human beings. Joseph Fletcher, widely known for his work entitled *Situation Ethics,* thought that Christian Ethics was simply ethics, and narrowed down the Christian warrant to a single imperative, the obligation to love the neighbor.[6]

Both Ramsey and Fletcher worked from the Christian tradition to the conclusion that morality was about love, or *agape,* and both considered the Christian imperative to love the neighbor to be central to the notion of morality for all human beings. But, as we shall see later, they worked out the implications of these commitments in very different, even opposing, ways.[7] The Society of Christian Ethics has almost a thousand members, each one of whom probably has some opinion on the relation of the words "Christian" and "Ethics." The spectrum of opinion is very wide. It is also three-dimensional, variegated, and nuanced. These differences often lie just below the surface of energetic debates about specific cases and issues.

So what is "Christian Ethics"? It is a term in common use that raises important questions. In this Foreword, the questions are formulated as the relation between moral behavior and Christian faith, and the emphasis is on disjunctions. The only thing that a reader can know for certain when picking up a book on Christian Ethics is that something will be said about Christianity, something about ethics, and something about how these two may, or even may not, relate to each other.

Yet the claim will be repeatedly made that this is a book about Christian Ethics. Questions the term raises will be addressed by discussing first morality as a social institution, then ethics as an intellectual discipline reflecting on morality, and finally consequentialism as a proposal for doing ethics in Christian perspective. An Afterword will concentrate on possible ways to think of connections, rather than disjunctions, between Christian faith and moral behavior.

Part One

The Institution of Morality

4. Morality as Social Institution

Morality . . . most obviously . . . is a social institution with a code of learnable rules.

—*Tom L. Beauchamp,* Philosophical Ethics

Morality is one of a number of social institutions that are necessary for the survival and flourishing of human life and for the preservation of global ecosystems that sustain that life.

In the Foreword, we have attempted in several ways to demonstrate the importance of specifying disjunctions between moral behavior and Christian faith. Significant problems arise if such disjunctions are ignored. We move now to a discussion of morality as a social institution. The assumption is that Christians need to be in civil conversation about moral matters with others than themselves, and that thinking about morality as a social institution can be an important step in that process.

Deciding to talk about morality as a social institution leaves open the question of the meaning of the word "moral." What is morality about? What distinguishes a moral issue from a legal issue, a political issue, or an issue of propriety or prudence? What makes a case study in morality different from one in etiquette or custom, or from a matter having to do with social location, gender, or generation? What is it that turns a technological problem or a business practice into a moral issue? Or do all such things have a moral edge, some moral content? When it is said that someone "takes the moral high ground," what is being said about that person or about the words or actions of that person? When a person says that an action is being taken "because it's the right thing to do," what does that mean, particularly when others consider it to be the wrong thing to do? Is there any reason to expect agreement among various groups or individuals about where that moral high ground is located or about what is the right thing to do? Are there any prospects in sight for a common morality?[1]

What are moral values as distinguished from, for example, religious, family, or personal values? Is there such a thing as moral development, and, if so, how is that development recognized and evaluated? Can it be measured? Can morality be taught, and, if so, how and under what circumstances? Or is morality something that can, as some say, only be "caught," only quietly instilled through significant life experiences with moral mentors or role models or cohesive families and communities?

Does morality have to do primarily with who a person is—with that person's character—or with what a person does—with that person's conduct? If it has to do with what a person does, is the primary reference point the adherence to universal moral rules, an educated sensitivity to the necessities of the situation at hand, or the willingness to work with projected or probable outcomes of one's behavior? These are not casual or arbitrary alternatives, but radically different options for understanding what morality is about. These alternatives will be explored in the next section of this book.

Must a moral act be an act of the will, a deliberate response to a non-negotiable moral imperative? Some people, including some ethicists, say so. Or do emotions and intuitions also play an important role? Some think morality has primarily to do with intuition. Or is it possible to behave morally with no conscious awareness whatever that one is making serious and difficult moral decisions? Might it even be a mark of the moral that the one who acts morally does so specifically in a spontaneous, rather than in a deliberate, way?

Are there immoral people, or are there only immoral acts done by human beings who should be regarded, by definition, as moral agents? If some people can be characterized as moral and others as immoral, how should this distinction be made?[2] Is morality an attribute of personal behavior, or does it have to do with social structures?[3] What shall we make of the title of the classic work by Reinhold Niebuhr, *Moral Man and Immoral Society*?[4]

Does morality have to do primarily with responsibilities toward other human beings? Can it be summed up with a term such as "neighbor-regard"? Or is morality a much larger reality, having to do with responsibilities toward the entire creation, as Oliver O'Donovan, for example, argues in *Resurrection and Moral Order*,[5] or James Gustafson in quite a different way in his *Ethics from a Theocentric Perspective*?[6]

It does not take a great deal of reflection to realize that the task of finding a generic understanding of morality is an extremely difficult one. There is no easy way to decide how best to use the word "morality." Someone could respond that morality has to do with actions that are right or wrong, good or bad. The problem is that there are right and wrong ways to hit a golf ball, and good and bad ways to manage one's investments. Does hitting golf balls or managing investments have anything to do with morality? One could argue a "yes" or "no" answer, but not on the basis of the mere use of the words "right" and "wrong," or "good" and "bad." How one thinks about golf balls and investments has, perhaps, something to do with morality. But if so, what?

If there are disagreements about responses to these kinds of questions, how can these disagreements be adjudicated? How can those who find themselves in dispute, not only about specific moral questions but about the nature of morality itself, engage one another in civil and productive conversation? It would be possible to qualify the opening statements by saying that morality has to do with what is *morally* right or wrong, good or bad. But that would be of no help. It simply begs the question. We would be back where we began, asking the meaning of the words "moral" and "morality."

The fact is that getting to a common understanding of morality, one to which almost everyone interested in talking about it could initially agree for the purpose of beginning a conversation, is extremely difficult. There is a common interest in morality, but that common interest in itself yields no common understanding of the term. The problem is exacerbated by the fact that disagreements are sometimes exceptionally passionate and uses of language extraordinarily confusing. It is a problem that needs intellectual work, but the importance of the problem is by no means only or even primarily intellectual. How people understand morality and choose to talk about it has serious repercussions for the survival and the flourishing of the human race and for the health of this planet on which we live.

An example of how difficult it is to get at a generic understanding of morality can be found in a splendid text by Tom L. Beauchamp.[7] After making some observations about "the concept of morality," Beauchamp offers a pluralist solution to the problem. He discusses four "marks of the moral." They are: (1) "a judgment, principle, or ideal is moral only if a person (or alternatively a society) accepts it as a *supremely authoritative or overriding* guide to action"; (2) "moral statements are distinguished from others by their *prescriptive form;* that is, they are action-guiding imperatives that do not *describe* states of affairs"; (3) moral statements are statements that should apply in a similar way to all people situated in relevantly similar circumstances; that is, moral statements must be universalizable; (4) "it is necessary for a moral action-guide to have some direct reference to *human flourishing,* to consider the *welfare of others,* or at least to be concerned with *harm and benefit to other persons."* Beauchamp concludes that there is no single set of marks that must always be present for a judgment, principle, or ideal to be moral and "even if none of the above four conditions is a necessary condition of morality, each may be *relevant* in mapping the geography of morality." Beauchamp offers this pluralist solution in a very tentative way. The entire discussion is couched in terms such as "highly likely," "reasonably assured," "a plausible hypothesis."[8]

Beauchamp's discussion is very helpful. One cannot get through it without sensing the difficulty of the task. The problem, however, with this pluralist solution is that it does not adequately take into account the fact that the different "marks" he suggests accompany different and even opposing understandings of what morality is about and of how one goes about the task of ethical reflection.

In Part 2 we shall be examining four methods that work with four different sets of criteria for understanding the nature of morality. For example, those who work with deontological methods will look for Beauchamp's mark #3 but not for mark #4. Those who work with teleological methods will look for mark #4 but not for mark #3. Deontologists and teleologists are equally interested in morality, but they disagree sharply on what morality is about. To list these four marks of the moral, and to say that if several are present there is probably a moral matter at hand, does not take with sufficient seriousness the opposing methodological viewpoints that exist about the meaning of the moral, and thus also about what marks of the moral ought to be given major consideration.

The suggestion here is that morality be understood as a social institution. People who disagree about almost everything else regarding morality may be able to agree that morality is a social institution, similar in many ways to other social institutions such as law, or religion, or government, or family, or education. The epigraph from Tom L. Beauchamp has been chosen specifically to indicate that disagreements that the author has with Beauchamp on related matters do not affect the common commitment to regard morality as a social institution.

Social institutions are clusters of commitments, obligations, regulations, expectations, values, habits, procedures, freedoms and limits, notions of things that are praiseworthy or blameworthy, memories and hopes that bind significant numbers of people together in various ways throughout long periods of time. Social institutions tend to be conservative. They exist prior to the arrival of individuals on the scene and they continue after these individuals depart. Social institutions are inherently somewhat amorphous. They are also porous, with elements of other institutions flowing in and out of them. Changes occur from time to time and from place to place, occasionally with great speed and force, but usually in a quiet and incremental way.

Without social institutions, societies could not exist. The human beings on this planet would be lonely individuals with violence as their only way to settle disputes. We would be not only "lower than the angels" (Heb. 2:7), but lower than other animals and even insects who have their own equivalents of societal structures intrinsic to their own survival. Human beings would be windowless monads in the words of Leibniz,[9] isolated islands in the words of John Donne.[10] If societies are going to survive and flourish, social institutions must be honored and nourished. One of these indispensable institutions is morality.

To understand morality as a social institution says nothing about the content of morality, nothing about what is to be considered morally right or wrong, good or bad, nothing about which actions should be required and which prohibited, nothing about what kind of human beings people should be if they want to be of good moral character. To suggest the understanding of morality as a social institution is a formal move. It is a small beginning. But it is a beginning. Everyone who uses the word "moral" in a way that expects others to listen and take notice ought to be able to agree that what is being talked about is something of social importance, potentially interesting to large numbers of people over long periods of time.

Such an understanding could, for example, help to bring disputants in the abortion debate into a somewhat neutral arena where serious conversation could at least begin. So-called pro-life and so-called pro-choice advocates in the abortion controversies ought to be able to agree that they are dealing with a moral issue. They disagree about where the moral question is located. So-called pro-life people believe that the moral issue is located in the protection of the life of the unborn child. So-called pro-choice people believe that the moral issue is located in the protection of the reproductive rights of women.

A good start might be that both groups could agree that everyone is for "life" and that everyone is for "choice," that the slogans of both parties are formulated by political power interests in addition to strictly moral motives. Yet both groups are vocal and politically active because they know they are dealing with a serious matter, that decisions made affect the future of society in significant ways. It is possible that disputants in this debate could agree that their disagreement has to do with something they consider to be "morality" and that morality can be usefully talked about as a social institution, an important set of threads in the fabric that helps to hold society together. That agreement would not guarantee a smooth and productive conversation. It might enable such a conversation at least to begin by locating the issue in the social institution of morality in which all parties involved share a common interest.

Morality is seldom taken to be a casual matter. Contrasting views come into conflict because at stake are social institutions that must exhibit some kind of cohesion. People with opposing views on capital punishment, details of welfare reform, their government's participation in a particular armed conflict, or proper uses of fertility technologies believe that they are raising the stakes in the dispute when they say that what they are dealing with is a moral issue. It is of no help at that point if each party simply assumes that its own position is obviously "the right thing to do." What is needed is some way to bring disputants into civil and constructive conversation.

The suggestion here is that a beginning, at least, may occur if both parties can agree that they are dealing with a moral issue, and that morality is an important social institution. Morality has to do, finally, not with arbitrary opinions of individuals, but with societal structures that are essential for the survival and flourishing of human life and the preservation of global ecosystems that make that life possible. The hope is that with this in mind disputants in serious moral controversies can become conversation partners in an atmosphere that begins with a common assumption and thus with some degree of mutual respect.

One of the things that makes conversation about moral matters difficult and delicate, but also intensely interesting and promising, is that morality is not an institution that can be totally isolated from other social institutions.

5. Morality and Other Social Institutions

It takes a village to raise a child.
    —*African proverb*

The institution of morality intersects, overlaps, can be confused with, and at times may conflict with other social institutions.

———

The African proverb "It takes a village to raise a child" is a concise reminder of the complexities and interconnections of social institutions. Hillary Rodham Clinton used it as a title for her best-selling book,[1] and it gave her an opportunity to promote causes and programs that she considers to be important, particularly for children, women, and families.

Not everyone was equally enthused. The title invited responses from people whose opinion is that too many government programs do more harm than good for the institution of the family. Some retorted by saying, "It takes a father and a mother to raise a child." These people believe that what is necessary for the healthy nurturing of children is that fathers and mothers take greater and more direct responsibility for raising the children they bring into the world. These people are not necessarily against government programs. They want to promote what they consider to be "family values."

It sounds like a legitimate disagreement, one that should lend itself to calm and constructive conversation. One could say that different emphases such as these often arise from conflicting opinions about social institutions. Opinions about the role of government in the United States range from minimalist notions, the call for less government and reduced taxes, to notions that regard the federal government as the chief agent of wealth redistribution and the primary benefactor of the disadvantaged. Everyone recognizes the importance of the family as social institution, but opinions vary widely about where to locate it in the context of other social institutions, how it can best function, and even how to define it. It is a mark of what some call "culture wars" that the term "family values" is a proud battle cry for some, for others an invitation to launch an attack on "the Christian Right."

Another social institution is education. It is thoroughly pervasive and totally essential for the flourishing of human life. It is also one around which swirl difficult and contentious opinions. Children must be educated. Societies cannot survive long unless they commit energy and resources to the institution of education. But how best to do this is a matter of endless controversy.

What about neighborhood schools, and busing, and magnet schools? Are public schools the place to redress centuries of racial discrimination? What about public and private schools, and who has access to a school of choice? What about vouchers? How about charter schools? Is home schooling a purely personal choice, or does the movement have public school consequences? How should local and state and federal concerns, controls, and resources be managed? Should teachers be required to take regular competence examinations? What about tenure for public school teachers and administrators? How about contributions from teachers' unions to political campaigns? How should the first amendment to the United States Constitution regarding the "non-establishment" and the "free exercise" of religion work in public classrooms?

What about sex education in public schools? Is value-free presentation of sexual materials possible? How much should parents have to say about what their children are taught, about texts that are used, about information to which their children are given access? Ought school nurses to distribute condoms? Should parents participate when their underage children receive abortion counseling?

The family is a fundamental social institution. So is education. But these are not monolithic, isolated, static realities. They are variegated, intertwined, fluid. And as soon as serious disagreements arise, people begin to say things that they believe are rooted in deep and basic moral commitments. When pressed to say why they think what they do about a family or an educational issue, regardless of positions taken, something that seems to have moral content soon enters the conversation. If such a conversation becomes heated, someone, no matter what is being advocated, is likely to come up with a comment like, "It's our moral duty." Morality is a social institution that intersects and overlaps with the institution of the family and the institution of education.

It has already been stated that the institution of government is thickly intertwined with family and education, and thus also with morality. Another social institution of particular interest is the law. People say to one another things such as "Live and let live" or "Let's agree to disagree" or "Who am I to judge?" or "It's her life to live." Such sentiments are important ways of getting along with one another, of reminding one another that there are limits to the interest people should have in the way others live their lives. The personal freedoms and civil liberties that are built into the constitutions and laws of democratic societies guarantee to individuals a wide range of life choices without fear of interference from other individuals or groups, including officers of the law or other government authorities.

The fact that personal freedoms and civil liberties are guaranteed does not mean that they are absolute or unlimited. Everyone knows that freedom of speech does not include the freedom to shout "Fire!" in a crowded theater when there is no fire, nor does freedom of assembly include the freedom to gather large numbers of people on a highway if there is no permit to do so. The right to bear arms does not allow a person to stockpile ground-to-air missiles in his garage, and the freedom to practice one's religion does not allow the ritual sacrifice of human beings on a religious altar. No freedom is entirely without limits, and no right is absolute. The law, from this perspective, is a delicate yet imperfect instrument that attempts to make appropriate compromises and balances between personal freedoms and social necessities.

The institution of morality functions in ways somewhat similar to the institution of law. Various kinds and degrees of pressure are brought to bear on people in order to encourage them to behave in ways that are considered to be moral and to discourage behavior that is considered to be immoral. These moral pressures function in softer ways than do legal restraints. One cannot be arrested or tried in court for the infraction of a moral rule alone. Yet moral pressures are real, often affect behavior, and sometimes are encoded into law.

Legality and morality are not identical, but they do have an impact on one another. It was probably a big mistake for the Republican presidential candidate Barry Goldwater, during the civil rights struggles of the 1960s, to declare, "You cannot legislate morality." The statement is only partially true. It is certainly the case that passing a law will not automatically turn a heart of stone into a heart of compassion. Yet civil rights and anti-discrimination laws can be designed in such a way that they discourage hate crimes and encourage generous behavior and, in the long run, tend to affect not only the manners but the morals of large groups of people.

Laws cannot turn liars into truth-tellers, but laws can encourage people to tell the truth on income tax returns and discourage them from lying under oath. Widespread notions of morality are often encoded in laws that not only penalize those who do not comply, but in so doing also assist people to behave in what many people consider to be acceptable ways. Law functions in both a punitive and an educative way, and the behavior that it helps to engender has something to do with what large numbers of people consider to be moral behavior.

Of course, it is also true that the institution of morality and the institution of law can come into conflict with each other. The most dramatic instances of such a conflict in the United States in relatively recent history were the struggles over civil rights and the Vietnam War. In both cases, large numbers of people took to the streets, often breaking laws, in order to protest laws and government activity that they considered to be morally unjust. Civil disobedience is usually driven by moral passion. In any given conflict, people will disagree on what legal changes need to be made to bring the law into congruence with what they consider to be the morally "right thing to do." In the continuing struggle over abortion, for example, people on both sides of the issue are willing to disobey laws that they believe encourage immoral behavior.

Etiquette is a social institution that seems at first to have nothing to do with morality. Learning how to use the salad fork properly, send regrets to a dinner invitation graciously, or allow a conversation partner to finish a comment without interruption cannot be equated with the moral importance of telling the truth or keeping a promise. Yet it is not for nothing that "manners and morals" are often combined in a single phrase. Etiquette may have to do with a large number of relatively unimportant things, but it also has to do with politeness, civility, thoughtfulness, straightforwardness, care, and consideration. It assists people to live together without unnecessary rancor, to hold tempers in control, to move somewhat smoothly through moments of potential trauma, and to avoid unnecessarily hurting people—even "rubbing people the wrong way," something that can turn healthy relationships into sour ones.

Etiquette sometimes becomes rather formally encoded into rules of procedure or codes of conduct. Within families, rules having to do, for example, with children asking to be excused from the dinner table, can be oppressive or liberating, depending on how they are thought about and observed. "Robert's Rules of Order" and similar parliamentary procedures are simply the formulating of rules of etiquette that help to assure a degree of decorum when people need to discuss their disagreements in productive ways. In such a situation, a "breach of etiquette" seems at least close to a move against accepted moral behavior.

The use of tobacco could be examined as a case study in the intertwining of social institutions. The entire economy of some early North American colonies was based on cotton and tobacco, and those economies soon became dependent upon slaves brought from Africa and purchased by plantation owners. The use of tobacco was an accepted pleasure, and it was accompanied by rituals and social graces. Long before the arrival of Europeans and Africans, Native Americans incorporated the use of tobacco into social practices and religious rituals. With the emancipation of women came also the acceptance of cigarette smoking by women, along with practices of etiquette that required a "gentleman" to light the cigarette of a "lady." Who from that era can forget the rendition by Frank Sinatra of the words, "A cigarette that bears the lipstick traces. . . . These little things remind me of you"?

Along with the roaring twenties and prohibition came the underground use of alcohol always accompanied by tobacco. Smoking was a constant presence in the movies. In World War II, cigarettes were a regular part of rations, and victorious allied troops handed out cigarettes along with candy bars to liberated civilians. The ever-present cigarette was a trademark for Edward R. Murrow, a media icon who died from complications of lung cancer.

All along the way, there were people who considered smoking tobacco to be a "filthy habit." Some called cigarettes "coffin nails." A popular western song went like this: "Smoke, smoke, smoke that cigarette. Puff, puff, puff, until you smoke yourself to death. Tell St. Peter at the Golden Gate that you hate to make him wait, but you just gotta have another cigarette."[2] There were no scientific studies available, but there were people who assumed that sucking smoke into one's lungs was not a very good idea.

Evidence began to accumulate that smoking cigarettes was, in fact, dangerous to one's health. Class action, state, and federal law suits have been common in the 1990s. Some states continue to receive federal support for raising tobacco. Other states have received massive financial settlements from tobacco companies to help compensate for financial losses due to medical costs related to cigarette smoking. Overseas markets for U.S. tobacco products are cause for bitter debates and possible lawsuits. Suddenly, cigars have become the accepted tobacco use of choice, and expensive cigars a conspicuous status symbol and display of wealth. Advertising agencies are accepting contracts both for and against the use of cigarettes.[3]

These suggestions about the use of tobacco as a case study are simply illustrative of the way in which social institutions interpenetrate one another. Tobacco use has to do with institutions of government, education, law, family, religion, etiquette—at least all of these. Intersecting all of them in one way or another are items that many people consider to be moral matters.

Because social institutions are both amorphous and porous, the question arises whether the institution of morality is so distinct from other social institutions that it can be useful to talk about a sharp distinction between the "moral" and the "non-moral."

6. Questions about the "Non-moral"

Teleological theories, then, make the right, the obligatory, and the morally good dependent on the nonmorally good.
—William Frankena, *Ethics*

Any useful understanding of morality must take into account its complex relationships with other social institutions.

It has already been observed that it is not unusual to hear a person say at some point in a conversation, "Well, now, that's a moral issue." The assumption that accompanies the remark is that there are moral issues and non-moral issues, and that moral issues ought to be thought about and handled in a different way from non-moral issues. The remark also usually carries the assumption that if it is a moral issue, it has to do with what is right and what is wrong, and this determination overrides all other considerations. When someone says, "Well, now, that's a moral issue," it is thought that the stakes are immediately raised exponentially.

An "amoral" person is a person with no sense of or sensitivity to morality. An "immoral" person is one who behaves in a way contrary to what most people think morality demands. "Non-moral" is a word different from both of these. It does not refer to a person, but to issues, problems, claims, values, judgments, obligations, and cases that are thought to have nothing to do with morality and to have no moral content.

Items designated as non-moral may be thought to be of importance, even of great importance, but are taken to be separable from moral matters. The assumption is significant because it is thought that building a case for a moral judgment involves a quite different set of presuppositions and procedures from those employed when making a case for a non-moral judgment. In a much-used standard ethics text, William Frankena makes this point by saying, ". . . morality must be distinguished from prudence."[1] He is saying that prudence may be an important criterion when making non-moral judgments, but prudence is not to be used when making moral judgments. His criticism of teleology, a system that we shall examine

31

later, is stated in the epigraph to this chapter. It is that teleology uses non-moral projected outcomes in the process of making moral decisions. Frankena is typical of many ethicists who work with a sharp distinction between the moral and the non-moral.

At first glance, it seems obvious that a great many things have nothing to do with morality. There are, for example, matters of taste. Some prefer a full-bodied red wine, others a lighter white. Some love to watch football games; others prefer ballet. It could be argued that the vast majority of choices we make have to do with matters of taste, preferences that are of no particular interest or importance to anyone but ourselves. It is understandable that some call such preferences "non-moral" matters.

It is also the case that some ethicists build entire systems of understanding moral behavior and ethical reflection on this sharp distinction between the moral and the non-moral. An example is William Frankena, already mentioned above. In his classic text, *Ethics,* he finishes his first chapter with a fascinating outline of sentences.[2] The sentences are very important to the argument of the book, and the categories into which the sentences are divided provide an indication of the content of the remaining chapters.

He calls all of these sentences "normative judgments." They are judgments because they are decisions or opinions rather than matters of fact. "In the United States, Christmas Day falls on December 25" is not a judgment, but a statement of fact. The judgments listed by Frankena are normative because they either state or imply recommendations. Some call such recommendations "action guides." If I say, "You ought to see this movie," it is a normative judgment because it makes a direct recommendation. If I say, "She walks gracefully," it is a normative judgment because by expressing this opinion, I am implying a recommendation that the person to whom I am speaking ought to consider emulating this graceful walk.

Frankena divides normative judgments into two major categories: "moral" and "non-moral." In each of these two categories he deals with "judgments of obligation," or direct recommendations, and with "judgments of value," or implied recommendations. This gives us four sets of sentences, and each of these he divides into another two parts, "particular" and "general." For example, he gives "We ought to keep our agreements" as an instance of a general normative judgment of moral obligation. He gives "That is a good car" as an instance of a particular normative judgment of non-moral value. Frankena's outline of sentences is fascinating and instructive. It is also provocative. Reflecting on the sentences one by one, and each in relation to others, is very hard but productive work.

Our purpose in this chapter is to raise questions about the use of the term "non-moral." William Frankena is an ethicist for whom the term is of fundamental importance, and he is a splendid representative of a class of ethicists whom we shall later come to know as "deontologists." The point here is that the sharp distinction of the "moral" from the "non-moral," insisted upon by Frankena and many others, does not adequately take into consideration the interpenetration of morality with other social institutions.

It is easy to understand the difference between the two sentences from Frankena mentioned above. "We ought to keep our agreements" sounds like a statement of moral obligation, and "That is a good car" sounds like a statement of non-moral value. However, as soon as we move from the construction of naked sentences into the complexities of real life, the distinction becomes blurred.

Is it always a moral obligation for every person to keep every agreement with every other person or group of persons? Some agreements are trivial. "Yes, that restaurant sounds great. I'll eat there sometime." It is a response to a recommendation. It is an agreement and thus a moral obligation. But the amount of time one has and the amount of money one cares to spend, even one's taste in food, may be taken as legitimate reasons to put it off indefinitely, never to get around to doing it. It is probably a moral obligation but one with very little weight.

When two people exchange marriage vows, they enter into an agreement that involves a life-long moral obligation to one another, to children who may be born to them, to society, to the institution of marriage. It is a moral obligation of great weight. Yet few think the agreement should be kept with no regard whatsoever to how the marriage works out. Most people think there are times when divorce may be a moral obligation. In the real world, what Frankena calls non-moral obligations and values invade what he calls moral obligations and values.

It is easy to understand that someone would call the sentence "That is a good car" a statement of non-moral value. But does the statement involve no moral judgment whatsoever? What kind of vehicle one needs, probable resale value, use of fuel, safety features, proper stewardship of financial resources, and many other considerations immediately come into play. Is it entirely obvious that there is no moral content anywhere in such considerations? We shall deal with this example more thoroughly in the following chapter.

Questions about the separation of the moral from the non-moral can be further illustrated by looking at two sentences, "He led a good life," and "He had a good life." They are both normative judgments and are analogous to two statements in Frankena's outline. The first is an illustration of what Frankena calls a moral judgment, the second an illustration of what he calls a non-moral judgment.

The wisdom of distinguishing the two is immediately evident. To say of someone, "He led a good life," is to commend that person for having spent his life in a useful way, for being conscientious about his decisions, for displaying honesty and integrity in his relationships, for behaving in what most people would consider to be a moral way. On the other hand, to say of a person, "He had a good life," is to say nothing about the morality of that person. It is to say, rather, that he enjoyed, perhaps, good health, was gifted with family and friends who loved and supported him, did not want for life's necessities, whatever it is that the person making the judgment considers to be the kind of life most people would like to have.

The distinction is important. People who lead very good lives can have very bad lives. It may be because of circumstances quite beyond the control of the person. The bad life one has may even be a rather direct result of the good life the person has led. Many have suffered the loss of freedom and health and have spent years in jail, or even suffered torture and death, because they have protested the evils of a corrupt government. Such people can be said to have had a bad life because they led a good life.

The opposite is also true. There are people who lead very bad lives, are dishonest in their business dealings, betray the very people who befriend them, think nothing of lying, and spend their time and energy doing what most people would consider to be immoral things. Yet some of these people have very good lives, if one thinks of a good life as one in which a person enjoys just about everything a person wants to enjoy.

Failing to make this important distinction between leading and having a good life can bring one to the not uncommon notion that the good prosper and the bad suffer. The idea has been around as long as have human beings and has existed in many forms. If we use our two sentences, this idea would say, "If you lead a good life, you will have a good life. If you lead a bad life, you will have a bad life." Common as this idea is, it is simply not the case. There is no automatic connection between leading a good life and having a good life.

But does that mean that there can be no possibility of any connection at all? Is it not the case that leading a good life may at times increase the probability that one will have a good life, and that leading a bad life may at times increase the probability that one will have a bad life? It is important to insist that there is no automatic or direct or guaranteed connection. But if a parent treats her children lovingly, is it not more likely that the children will treat her lovingly? If I treat others with respect and dignity, is it not, under most conditions, more likely that they will treat me with respect and dignity? If I lead a life of moderation, paying attention to diet and exercise and sleep, do I not increase the probability that I will enjoy a healthier life than if I disregard all known rules for healthy living? Leading a good life does not have absolutely nothing to do with having a good life. It may perhaps actually increase the probabilities of having a good life. To call "He led a good life" a purely moral judgment, and "He had a good life" a purely non-moral judgment does not seem adequately to take into consideration possible overlappings and connections between the two.

Further, when one looks at actual individuals in real life, it quickly gets even more complex. Nobody leads a perfect life, and nobody has a perfect life. When making a judgment about how a person has led her life, we are accustomed to take into consideration what kind of a life she has had. We tend to make allowances for a person brought up in a severely impoverished and abusive environment. We may say, "She did very well with what she had to work with." We do the same when speaking about someone brought up in a household full of love and advantages. We may say, "He took these gifts and squandered them," even though the life he led was not particularly blameworthy. So-called non-moral ingredients regularly feed into so-called moral judgments.

Frankena says that morality, of course, must be distinguished from prudence. It is part of a total argument that prudence is a criterion appropriate for non-moral decisions, but specifically not for moral decisions. The argument in this book is that this distinction is too clean, too sharp, too divorced from the actual complexities of life. It is, in general, a good thing to plan carefully for the future. People who lead good lives usually live prudent lives. It is surely not a virtue to live one's life carelessly. The prudent practice of regular saving and investing may make it possible for a person to be a benefactor to people in need. So-called non-moral judgments may be so intertwined with so-called moral judgments that in some cases the latter may be impossible apart from the former.

There are ways of understanding morality and ethical reflection that insist on an absolutely sharp division between the moral and the non-moral. The distinction is understandable and in some ways important. The argument in this book is that this sharp distinction is finally unhelpful, because it does not adequately reflect the many relationships of morality with other social institutions.

If all of these relationships to other social institutions are taken seriously, it may be that questions about the existence of purely non-moral judgments of value and obligation may drive us to quite a different way of talking about morality itself. It may be that we should talk about morality in terms such as "degrees of moral density."

7. Degrees of Moral Density

Moral codes must teach a moral law which corresponds to the order of reality in its differentiation and complexity.
—*Oliver O'Donovan,* Resurrection and Moral Order

The real world may be better addressed by speaking about degrees of moral density, rather than by attempting to distinguish sharply the moral from the non-moral.

———————

The position presented here is that morality is a social institution that intersects, overlaps, can be confused with, and at times may conflict with other social institutions. When the many relationships between morality and other social institutions are taken into account, serious questions arise about the commonly held notion that it is not only possible, but necessary, to distinguish sharply moral from non-moral matters.

When one probes, for example, questions about going to the opera and about taking care of one's ailing mother, it soon becomes apparent that details begin to flow in and out of one another in such a way that it is difficult to conclude that the first item has only non-moral content and the second only moral content. It may, however, be possible to say that the obligation to take care of one's ailing mother has a far greater degree of moral density than an obligation to go to the opera. On the other hand, if one is totally exhausted from the demands of caregiving, and if an evening at the opera is likely to bring necessary refreshment to one's soul so that one can resume the task, it may well be that going to the opera becomes a moral obligation of significant weight. Not to spend that evening at the opera may put in jeopardy one's ability to continue to be a caregiver to one's ailing mother.

Let us look at another example. "You ought to buy a new car" is a type of sentence that William Frankena would give as an example of a non-moral normative judgment of particular obligation.[1] The obligation is "particular" because it is addressed to a single person and gives a single recommendation. There is no general imperative for everyone to buy a new car. Frankena's primary commitment here is that the entire consideration is not a moral matter. Such things as buying new cars can be settled on prudential grounds alone, that is, on the basis of what one considers to be the wisest thing to do, without any reference to moral criteria. It means that it would be inappropriate to address such a question with queries about the morally right or wrong thing to do. But does this make sense in the real world? It does not seem to take a great deal of reflection to see that what most people think of as moral considerations quickly begin to invade the matter of buying a new car.

Anyone told by another person to buy a new car has a right to ask, "Why?" That question leads quickly to others. The car is an inanimate object, and the money used in such a transaction is simply a medium of exchange, but the potential buyer is a human being. This person's humanity is deeply set in a matrix of moral accountability that penetrates communities of people whose flourishing and even existence depend upon the nourishing of many social institutions. When the potential buyer takes seriously the moral core of her humanity and her importance as a moral agent, her mind begins to wander in and out of, and around the edges of, questions that seem to carry some moral content.

How efficient is the car she is now driving in its use of irreplaceable fossil fuels? How well have safety considerations been factored into new designs, and what protections can she expect for herself and her passengers, and those in other vehicles on the road? Are potential gains in these matters, if a new car is purchased, significant? How can some kind of cost/benefit analysis be carried out on the safety question, acknowledging that there is risk every time one gets behind the wheel, and that absolute safety cannot be achieved? Ought she to consider where a car and its parts are manufactured and assembled, and what economic implications for workers and families, in one's own country and abroad, such economic considerations may have? Is the car designed and manufactured to last as long as possible, and how does this factor into her own needs and to resale value and safety for the next owner?

The question for the person told to buy a new car is not just what kind of a car to buy, but whether to buy a car at all. How much do I need this car? Ought I to use the money for some purpose other than the purchase of a new car? Would looking for an appropriate used

vehicle be a more responsible action? Ought I to factor into my decision the anticipated pleasure I would derive from owning and driving
a new car? The questions go on. For anyone with some awareness of
moral accountability, the buying of a car immediately raises questions that it would seem strange to think about as purely non-moral
matters. The problem here is whether there is a way of understanding morality that can yield more helpful language, presuppositions,
and procedures than does the attempt to draw a sharp dividing line
between the "moral" and the "non-moral."

Perhaps there is a way. Let us consider the use of a term such as
"degree of moral density." Such a term would honor the integrity of
the institution of morality and at the same time acknowledge its
many and complex relationships to other social institutions. Using
such a term would require abandoning the idea that there is any such
thing as a normative judgment of value or obligation that is either
purely moral or purely non-moral. It would assert that there is probably no normative judgment totally devoid of moral content, yet
that some judgments carry greater moral content than others. These
differences in moral content may be expressed by referring to varying degrees of moral density.

For example, we have tried to show that there are considerations
that almost everyone would recognize as moral considerations buried
not so deeply below the surface of the question of whether to buy a
new car. Yet it is obvious that the question of whether to buy a new
car is not the moral equivalent of the question of whether to participate in a plan to profit from the laundering of money derived from
the sale of illegal drugs. The latter is considerably weightier than the
former. The moral density of a judgment about one's daily exercise
may be quite thin, and that about how to vote in a referendum on the
legalization of physician-assisted suicide very thick. Yet once the
presence of moral content in each is acknowledged, the difference
becomes a difference in degree.

Nothing in life can be bracketed off into an arena totally devoid
of moral content, and nothing can be isolated into a realm of the
purely moral. Presuppositions and procedures for dealing with serious matters may well need to be adjusted to what one decides about
the degree of moral density the matter carries. But if the assumptions argued here are correct, no sharp distinction in presuppositions

and procedures can be made on the basis of a sharp distinction between "moral" and "non-moral" matters.

The conceptualization of morality here proposed under the rubric of "degrees of moral density" can also be expressed in other ways. One example is the suggestion of Oliver O'Donovan that we talk about the pluriformity of the moral field. He writes:

> The dilemma arises because the moral field is pluriform. It does not arise out of the adequacy or inadequacy of the moral code which the agent may happen to have been taught, or to have formulated for himself. . . . For pluriformity is not an accident or defect of codes. . . . The order of reality holds together a multitude of different kinds of moral relation, and orders them without abolishing their differences. Moral codes must teach a moral law which corresponds to the order of reality in its differentiation and complexity.[2]

We shall have occasion later to speak about morality and ethics in the context of field theory. At the moment, it is only necessary to recognize that there is a variety of terminology available that seeks to make the same case. One could also, for example, speak of "degrees of moral gravity" rather than of "degrees of moral density." One could talk about degrees of moral importance, or of weight, or of thickness.

This way of thinking about morality in terms of degree may make some Christians nervous. They may conclude that degrees of moral density imply degrees of human sinfulness. The worry is understandable, but can be traced to a confusion between immorality and sin. In Christian discourse, the two have something to do with one another, but they are not identical. They have different points of reference and different contexts of meaning.

"Sin" is a word that Christians use in reference to God. It refers to a state, a condition, in which all people exist. Sinfulness is indivisible. It is a sickness that is pervasive throughout the entire self. In relation to God, Christians say, everyone is equally sinful and equally in need of God's total redemptive gift. There are no degrees of sinfulness, and there are no degrees of God's forgiveness. The question becomes more problematic when one moves from the condition of sinfulness to specific acts of sin. Christians confess that, in addition to being sinful, they commit acts of sin, and it is not uncommon to specify these acts. Sometimes, actual sins seem to be graduated in degrees. An example would be the confession, "We have sinned against you by thought, word, and deed." A word of hatred against me may be more harmful than a thought marked by hate, and a hateful deed more harmful still. Yet, as Jesus points out in the "antitheses" of Matthew 5, every sin, regardless of its effect, is an indication of our sinfulness and need for daily forgiveness.

"Morality" is a word whose proper reference is to a human social institution. We shall talk later about whether one person may be said to have a better moral character than another, or to be a more moral person. The point in this chapter is that some issues, claims, values, obligations, or duties have greater moral weight or greater moral importance than do others. Talking about degrees of moral density does not in any way infringe upon the Christian confession about the total way that sinfulness penetrates every human life, and the total need of every human being to become a recipient of God's grace. It is true that in common use immorality and sin are often talked about in confusing ways. This does not mean that what is being said here about degrees of moral density is a threat to the Christian confession about the equality of sinfulness present in all people.

The claim that morality is a social institution that intersects, overlaps, can be confused with, and sometimes conflicts with other social institutions calls into question the sharp separation between the moral and the non-moral. The use of a term such as "degrees of moral density" may help to address morality as it exists in the real world. It may also help conversation partners in moral disputes to come to serious disagreement.

8. Coming to Moral Disagreement

"Disagreement," noted the great American Catholic pluralist John Courtney Murray, "is not an easy thing to reach." The aim of this book is to reach disagreement.

Jean Bethke Elshtain, Democracy on Trial

Constructive conversation in moral disputes often fails to materialize, because disputants tend to think that the problem lies elsewhere than in genuine disagreement.

One might think that the goal of ethical reflection and moral discourse would be that everyone involved would come to the point of agreement. It could be that agreement might be among some set of distant hopes. The fact is, however, that if agreement is too strong and too urgent an expectation, it almost certainly will not occur. Opinions about things that people consider to be moral matters are usually deeply felt and firmly held. They are not easily compromised, brushed aside, or explained away. At the very least, people in moral disputes want their opinions to be taken seriously, and in order for that to happen, it must be recognized that disagreements can be both genuine and substantial. Productive work toward possible agreement can begin only when there is a mutual acknowledgment that serious disagreements exist and will be honorably addressed. Getting to this point is often extremely difficult and time-consuming.

A reason that people often find it difficult to imagine that there is genuine disagreement about moral matters is that morality is thought to be a distinguishing mark of the human. Animals, even insects, may exhibit hostile or benevolent behavior toward members of their own and other species. Those who have spent great amounts of time studying primates have documented in detail similarities between their behaviors and ours. But few people would consider using moral language to describe these similarities, and there is no evidence that animals other than human beings engage in ethical reflection and moral debate. Those species of birds who mate for life are not considered to be morally superior to dogs who do not, and those animals that take care of their young for long periods of time are not considered to be of better moral character than those who quickly allow their young to fend for themselves. If a research person writes about altruism in fruit flies, the word "altruism" is used not as a moral commendation, but as a biological description. A dog may be gentle or ill-tempered, but these character traits are not designated as morally praiseworthy or blameworthy. The institution of morality seems to be treated by virtually everyone as a strictly human social institution.

Arguments can be made that the distinguishing mark of the human has to do with brain size and function, language, collective memory and historical awareness, or even with manual dexterity. Christians claim that the distinguishing mark of the human is a special relationship to God, in whose "image" human beings were created on the "sixth day," after everything else, including all other living creatures, was in place. Religious people, whatever their notions about God, may claim that only human beings have a "spiritual dimension," and that this is the distinguishing mark of the human.

There are many different ways that people think about the uniqueness of human beings in the cosmic order. There are also people who with good reason want to emphasize our mutual relatedness to and interdependence with all other things and all other creatures. There is a vast spectrum of opinion, with many variations along the way, having to do with how human beings fit into the whole of nature, the created order, reality, or the cosmos. How one expresses the "whole" often has something to do with how one expresses the place of the human within the whole.

Nevertheless, the most common understanding of the distinguishing mark of the human is that it is only human beings who are moral creatures, make moral choices and decisions, think about behaviors in moral terms, and consider themselves to be moral agents.

This notion of morality is so close to the marrow and fiber of our self-understanding as human that it is sometimes difficult to imagine another person in fundamental disagreement with us about what that humanity, and that morality, entail. People tend to think that to take seriously another's moral disagreement is to call into question one's own fundamental morality, which implies calling into question one's own fundamental humanity.

Thus the initial reaction that often occurs in moral disputes is one of amazement. Disagreements in many other areas of life may be understandable, but it is thought that human beings certainly should be able to agree on what is morally right and wrong. When it comes to moral matters, we are not talking about peripheral opinions, but about fundamental realities of human life. When someone appears to disagree on a serious moral issue, there may be a slow shaking of the head, or a roll of the eyes, or even a vocal "How can you possibly say that?" The initial reaction is that there must be some mistake, that nobody could seriously disagree about something so basic and so obvious. Since it is thought that no legitimate opinion is there to be discussed, no discussion takes place. Instead, various attempts to point out what is taken to be an unfortunate mistake come into play.

Sometimes the amazement gets expressed in a blatantly *ad hominem* way. The one who begs to differ, to have an opinion taken as a serious disagreement, is dismissed as being in some way so influenced by personal circumstances that he is incapable of making an independent judgment. Depending on the etiquette level of the exchange, a person might say, "You just don't get it, do you?" Or one hears remarks such as, "Where have you been living, in a cave?" or "If you lived where I live, you'd understand," or "Get real, will you?" More polite responses may assume that the person who disagrees is quite simply and directly led to a moral opinion by prejudices resulting from gender, family history, economic status, religious affiliation, or even by one's profile on the Myers-Briggs Type Indicator test. The assumption is that the other person need not be taken seriously because her opinion is merely a reflection of her biases.

Or it may be thought that the other person needs a consciousness-raising experience. The idea is that the other person, of course, knows that my position is correct, but unfortunately that knowledge is buried deeply under a cluster of assumptions and emotions that do not allow it to be recognized and expressed. Perhaps this person has led too sheltered a life and is through no fault of his own experientially deprived. Since the apparent disagreement must be only superficial, raising the truth to consciousness through contact with appropriate experiences will take care of the problem.

Another device is to assume that the problem is a lack of good mental health on the part of the person who disagrees on a moral

issue. It is assumed that the apparent disagreement is due to a pho-
bia of some sort, an irrational fear of "the other" or of the unfamiliar.
When a strong disagreement is expressed, the person addressed may
say, "What are you afraid of?" or "Why do you feel so threatened?"
Or the person may simply be told to relax. There are people who
think that everyone who disagrees with them does so because he or
she is too "uptight."

For example, if a person has reached a serious conclusion that
holds that heterosexual marriage is the only appropriate place for
mutual genital activity, it is not likely that any constructive conversation will result if that conclusion is automatically attributed to
"homophobia." The very hard task of working through serious moral
disagreement is avoided by assuming that the person who thinks
there is a disagreement is simply expressing anxieties and other inappropriate feelings due to inadequate experience in healthy relationships. Whatever the cause, the assumption is that the problem is not
disagreement, but some lack of mental health in the one who thinks
there is a disagreement. The person who thinks there is disagreement is thought to need therapy or a serious commitment to working through his personal problems.

Coming to moral disagreement is also blocked when it is decided
that the problem is the other person's lack of compassion or some
other essential human quality. The assumption is that there must be
a serious character flaw in anyone who questions my way of attempting to help people in need. It is thought that compassion is so monolithic, so unidirectional, that it leads automatically and directly to
solutions to even the most difficult social and economic complexities, and that what needs to be done is simply to preach compassion
to the person who obviously lacks it.

In addition to these and other devices, there are some special ways
in which Christians sometimes attempt to avoid coming to serious
moral disagreement. Some like to say, "I have really prayed about
this." The implication is that the other person would obviously agree
if sufficient time had been spent in prayer. Or some Christians quote
a passage from the Bible, thinking that this will immediately
enlighten the other person. Difficulties and differences in biblical
interpretation are often simply ignored. Or some say, "The Lord has
made it so clear to me." The thought is that if you would only listen
to the Lord, you would get the same answer as I have. The fact that

these ways to avoid coming to disagreement are often deeply set in religious as well as moral commitments may make it, in some cases, particularly difficult for Christians to enter into constructive conversation about serious moral matters.

It is true, of course, that some people need consciousness-raising experiences, or better mental health, or a good dose of compassion. It is true that some Christians do not pray for guidance, are not diligent in their Bible reading, are not open to the prompting of God's Spirit. It is also true that some disagreements are only apparent, that a little careful clarification will show that essential agreement exists. It is also true that some moral disagreements are trivial, that they lack sufficient moral density to warrant conversation. But in some of these cases, it may be that the disagreement is specifically about how trivial or how important the issue is, what degree of moral density it carries. A moral issue is not trivial just because one partner in a dispute says it is.

In any case, it is a fact that equally intelligent and educated people who are also equally experienced, sensitive, and compassionate can and do disagree about moral matters of great importance. These disagreements are probably as widespread and as deeply felt and firmly held among people who are Christians as among those who are not. Nothing constructive can take place until this fact is squarely faced, that people who are moral equals can and do have important disagreements about moral questions, issues, and cases.

So it is necessary, however difficult it may be, to structure our reflection about morality in such a way that it is possible to recognize genuine disagreement when it does appear and to deal with it in a civil and productive manner. The discipline of ethics is careful reflection about moral matters, so careful that it allows the recognition of moral disagreements and provides procedures and mechanisms for constructive and civil conversation about them. Coming to disagreement in serious moral disputes is both necessary and difficult. It is an essential first step. How the conversation proceeds will depend, in large part, upon what skills in ethical reflection conversation partners bring to the table. We move now to a discussion of the discipline of ethics.

Part Two

The Discipline of Ethics

9. Morality and Ethics

An important distinction must be made between moral decision-making and ethical analysis. . . . Ethics . . . is clearly related to intelligent moral decision-making, but is not identical with it.
  —*Robin Gill,* A Textbook of Christian Ethics

Ethics is an intellectual discipline that seeks to understand, reflect upon, and speak helpfully about the institution of morality.

—————

The subtitle of this book and the titles of the first two sections make it clear that an important distinction is being drawn between the words "morality" and "ethics." Important as this distinction is for the doing of ethics, it must be acknowledged that the distinction is not always, or even generally, observed in common speech. When someone asks, "What ever happened to ethics in government?" the person is usually not asking what happened to careful reflection about morality in government, but rather what happened to morality itself. When someone says, "He has no ethics at all," the comment usually does not refer to this person's lack of ability to think clearly and speak helpfully about morality. It usually refers to a judgment about the person's basic disregard for moral behavior.

Although there is a common tendency to merge uses of the words "morality" and "ethics," it should be clear that there is nothing strange or unusual about the use of different terms to distinguish the doing of something from the examination and study of that doing. A person may be a very successful and honored politician without ever having studied political science or law or the history of government. A person may be an important political scientist whose publications are widely read and may never have served in public office or even worked in a political campaign. Being a politician and being a political scientist are two different things. There are many important ways in which the two activities may relate to each other, but that does not make the distinction unimportant. In a similar way, the task of literary criticism is not the same as that of writing a novel, theories of child development not identical to the task of raising a child.

A place to locate the distinction in a Christian context is to point to the difference between the words "faith" and "theology." Faith is an activity of the total self. It is receiving the gracious gift of forgiveness, believing in Jesus as Lord and Savior, turning one's back on evil, and turning toward the will of God. However it is described, faith has to do with one's total existence. Many persons of profound faith may have never heard the word "theology," know nothing about it, and need not to know about it in order to be people of faith. Theology is an intellectual discipline that seeks to understand faith (or, as some theologians think, to argue that faith cannot be understood), to speak about faith in a helpful way, to address questions that faith raises. One might hope that most Christian theologians would be people of faith, yet it is possible to spend one's life doing theology, to know a great deal about faith, and yet to believe that none of it is true. Christian faith and Christian theology ought, and usually do, have a great deal to do with one another, but they are not identical. The distinction is of critical importance.

We are making this distinction between the doing of something and the examination and study of the doing of something by maintaining a distinction between morality and ethics. "Morality" is used to refer to the character and conduct of people and groups of people in actual life situations. Morality refers to how people behave in what is determined to be moral matters, and we are calling this "the institution of morality." "Ethics" is used to refer to an intellectual task of attempting to understand morality, to speak about it helpfully, to sort out and arrange presuppositions and procedures for arriving at conclusions to moral questions and issues. We are calling this "the discipline of ethics."

Although frequently unobserved in casual usage, the distinction is almost universally regarded as important in academic institutions. It is "ethics," not "morality," that is used to refer to the academic discipline at which teachers and scholars work. There may be a college or university that offers a course in morality, but it seems strange, at best, to give tests and grades in morality. It would be like giving tests and grades in faith. Morality is more important than ethics, and faith is more important than theology. But morality and faith are not appropriate subjects for tests, grade scores, or the award of academic honors.

This entire book is about Christian Ethics. We were doing ethics
in Part 1 when we attempted to understand morality as a social institution. We are doing ethics in this section when we attempt to
understand ethics as an intellectual discipline. We shall still be
doing ethics in Part 3 when we attempt to suggest a particular set of
presuppositions and procedures for reaching conclusions about moral
matters and for engaging in conversation about those conclusions.
The writing or reading of a book is not the living of a life, but it is
hoped that it might be of some help in the living of a life. Such help,
if it occurs, will have to do with ethics, with reflecting on and con-
versing about moral matters rather than with direct moral counsel or
the recommendation of answers to moral questions.

To say that ethics is an intellectual discipline is simply to sharpen
the distinction between the institution of morality and the discipline of ethics. It does not mean that in order to do ethics, one must
be intellectually gifted, or even intellectually inclined. It means,
rather, that ethics is intellectual work. It is done with reflection and
conscious expression, with sentences and paragraphs. The morality
upon which it reflects is done with the total self. It is, in fact, specifically to guard the fact that morality is not appropriately spoken of
as an intellectual task, that the word "intellectual" is reserved for the
discipline of ethics.

It can be confusing. Carol Gilligan has argued in her pioneering
work, *In a Different Voice,*[1] that women tend to make decisions,
including moral decisions, using a fuller range of their total
human capacities than do men, who tend to approach problems in
a more strictly intellectual way. Sidney Callahan's work, *In Good
Conscience: Reason and Emotion in Moral Decision Making,*[2] argues
that the emotions should and do play an important role in moral
decision-making. Sometimes the point is made by contrasting
"holistic" and "rational," or by referring to "right brain" activity and
"left brain" activity. Sometimes "creative thinking" is contrasted to
"linear thinking." There has been a great deal of research and discussion, and there is an impressive body of literature having to do with
these contrasts.

There is no question that legitimate arguments can be made
about some different ways in which women and men, in general,
tend to do things. It is certainly the case that emotions ought not to

be ignored when making moral decisions. The point here is that it is important to reserve the word "ethics" for the task of reflecting upon and speaking helpfully about morality, and that this must be done in the context of serious and respectful conversation with people with whom one disagrees. The initial point in such a conversation cannot be to persuade but rather to understand one's own position as well as that of one's conversation partner, and this often requires very hard intellectual work.

To say in a moral dispute that one thinks the way one does because one is male or female may or may not be the case. But this fact must then, after being stated, be subject to some further criteria that apply to both female and male, to our common humanity, if the conversation is going to go anywhere. I cannot expect to advance a conversation about a moral disagreement by saying how strongly I feel about my opinion, or by claiming that my emotional response to the issue is more legitimate than the emotional response of the person with whom I disagree. It may or may not be true, but the doing of ethics must seek to advance conversations about moral disputes, not to put an end to them.

Etymologically, words such as "morality" come from a Latin root, and words such as "ethics" come from a Greek root. It is all very interesting and worth pursuing, but a thorough analysis of the ancient meanings of these roots and the various routes they have traveled through the history of various languages is not essential at this point. Our primary concern is not etymology, but usage, and how to be as clear as possible about what we are doing.

We want to be clear about how we are using the terms "morality" and "ethics." But it is also important to note that there are many other terms related to the same two roots that are often used in talk about these matters. Words are living things with fluid and some-times multiple meanings. We have already pointed to quite different meanings of the word "ethics," as used in casual and in technical language. What follows is a brief attempt to suggest some meanings for some important words often used in the discipline of ethics.

We have already had occasion to mention the terms "amoral" and "immoral," in connection with questions raised about the term "non-moral." The words "immoral" and "unethical" have identical meanings. Both refer to a person or persons whose behavior is considered blameworthy. It is difficult to imagine anyone using the term "unethical" to refer to a person who does not know anything about the discipline of ethics. When used as adjectives, the terms "ethical" and "moral" have identical meanings. When used as adjectives about issues or cases, they mean that this issue or case probably has significant moral content. When used as adjectives about people, the words are used to commend the character and conduct of the person or persons being talked about. A "moral" or an "ethical" person is referred to as such because the speaker wants to indicate an opinion that this is a good person who does good things.

It is quite different with the words "moralist" and "ethicist." The first is almost always a pejorative term, used about people who, in the opinion of the speaker, are not only overly scrupulous about their own behavior, but overly judgmental about the behavior of others. When the term becomes an adjective, it is even more clear. To say of someone that he is "moralistic" is to say he is overly scrupulous and judgmental. It is entirely different from saying that someone is a "moral" person. An "ethicist," on the other hand, is clearly one who works at the discipline of ethics, as a physicist works at the discipline of physics. The term "ethicist" has nothing to say about the person's character or conduct, rather only about what that person does as a craft or a hobby or a profession.

Many words are attached to the word "ethics" in various contexts. The term "Christian Ethics" has already been discussed, along with some of the issues that the mere combining of these two words raises. The field of "philosophical ethics" is as broad and as variegated as is Christian Ethics, even though there are commonalities to be found among philosophers who work in this field. Sometimes people who work in philosophical ethics are called "moral philosophers," and people who work in theological ethics "moral theologians." There is a field known as "religious ethics." An ethicist may specialize in "Buddhist ethics," "postmodern ethics," "liberation ethics," "feminist ethics," or "Lutheran ethics." The qualifier in each case refers to some restricted yet still broad commitment of the one doing the ethics, but does not in any case refer to a monolithic body of either presuppositions or procedures for doing ethics, nor to a body of conclusions to moral questions. All of these qualifying adjectives simply narrow the arena in which ethical reflection is carried out.

Radically differing procedures and conclusions exist in every identifiable group.

Terms such as "business ethics," "legal ethics," and "medical ethics" are more ambiguous. They may refer to a body of procedures and conclusions to which the writer of a text or the teacher of a course may come after considerable reflection. They may refer to ways in which ethical reflection may take place in a particular arena of moral issues. They may also refer to professional codes of conduct by which professional groups, or even specific companies, law firms, or medical clinics, may seek to monitor their representatives for the sake of maintaining public trust. The word "ethics," in each of these cases, probably has more to do with what these groups consider to be moral behavior than with reflection upon behavioral options or upon morality as such. That is, when the word "ethics" is used in reference to a specific code of conduct, it probably has more to do with the institution of morality than with the discipline of ethics.

A term that the reader is not likely to encounter, but of which she should be aware, is "meta-ethics." It is used primarily by philosophers, and it designates the examination of the language used in moral discourse and ethical reflection. It can be thought of as the extension of "language philosophy" into the field of ethics. There is a large body of literature on meta-ethics, but one example is Richard Hare's *The Language of Morals*.[3] Hare does extensive work on the uses of, for example, the indicative and the imperative moods in moral discourse. He argues convincingly that in common usage a sentence set in the indicative mood may express a moral imperative, and one set in the imperative mood an indicative judgment that may or may not relate directly to a moral matter.

This is a book about Christian Ethics, but one that seeks to be in conversation with ethics done by people who do not share Christian commitments. The primarily descriptive work in the first two sections is designed to be applicable to the full range of specialized areas of ethics and to the many points of view of those who do ethics. The third, primarily constructive or normative, section is offered to the reader for consideration as a gathered position for doing ethics in a Christian context.

10. The Importance of Methodological Clarity

But why, Dad?

It is important for a person's own moral health, but also for conversation with others, to know why one thinks what one does about moral matters. Ethics has to do with that "why."

———

Responsible parents begin the moral education of their children at a very early age. As children begin to mature, they begin to wonder about some of the moral counsel they receive. They begin to ask, "Why?" "Because I said so" is at times an appropriate response, but it does not go very far to answer the child's question, and grows less and less useful as the child develops her own mind and life. When dealing with adults, "Because I said so" is almost never an appropriate response to a person who asks why a particular moral view is held or why a particular moral decision has been made.

The discipline of ethics can be useful in quiet personal conversations, such as that between a parent and a child, or among several adult friends. It can also be useful in large situations where issues with great moral density are at stake. One way to understand the discipline of ethics is to think of it as a tool for bringing into civil and productive conversation people who have significant disagreements about important moral concerns. Because these concerns often carry a heavy emotional load and are frequently expressed with some passion, civil and productive conversation does not come easily. Without some ability to stand back from one's views long enough to realize that they are, in fact, viewpoints or judgments and not simple truths, such conversation is at best extremely difficult.

In cases where differences are perceived to be both irreconcilable and intolerable, the lack of reflective skills drives disputants quickly to the use of various kinds of force. This force may begin with the raising of one's voice, but not infrequently degenerates into verbal combat. When the debate has to do with large groups of people and involves an issue of concern across geographical and other borders, the verbal combat can turn into a culture war, in which all sorts of political force come to be used to defeat the opponents, almost at any cost. Abortion is such an issue. Another illustration is the Vietnam War, which seriously divided people in the United States. Various issues swirling around affirmative action and welfare reform are similar flash points. Ethics in this context may be understood as a cluster of conversation helps that can at least delay and in some cases make unnecessary the use of force.

The question is not how two parties can compromise or how techniques of conflict resolution can be applied. Compromise and conflict resolution are extremely important, particularly in political debates and, for example, labor-management relations. Politics may be the art of the possible and compromise may be that without which politics is not possible. Morality, on the other hand, is not simply politics, and moral disputes do not often lend themselves to mere compromise. In fact, morality is defined by many precisely as having to do with matters on which one does not compromise. It is thought that one ought not to compromise on the truth and one ought not to compromise on that which is the morally right thing to do. Morality is something many believe by definition ought to override all other considerations, specifically the temptation to compromise, to put "politics" above "principle."

Ethics is no guarantee that a moral disagreement that was perceived to be intolerable will become tolerable, or that what was thought to be irreconcilable will become reconcilable. But it is a discipline that can serve to cool tempers, order conversational priorities and procedures, encourage respect for the opinions of others, and help to bring to light and expression commitments that lie behind conclusions on a particular moral case or issue. Genuine conversation can sometimes lead to understanding, and understanding can sometimes lead to a degree of tolerability or reconcilability that prior to serious conversation had been thought impossible.

What the discipline of ethics can provide, in addition to help for individuals and groups in arriving at positions on moral issues, is help in discovering and stating clearly the reasons for arriving at those positions. A position taken on a particular moral issue can be called a moral judgment. The way in which the judgment has been arrived at can be called an ethical method. This section of the book deals with the discipline of ethics and does so by describing four alternative methods for the doing of ethics. The claim being made is that there are four great methodological groups that provide intellectual structures and procedures for arriving at and evaluating moral judgments.

The claim sounds strange. It sounds strange to people who have never considered the possibility of methodologically distinct ways of reaching and evaluating moral judgments. People who are certain that there is nothing to talk about when it comes to morality, that the only problem is to do the right thing, or to follow one's conscience, or to do what one knows Jesus would do, will have difficulty generating sufficient interest to struggle with methodological options in ethics. Considering the possibility that a moral opponent may be "right" includes the possibility that one may oneself be "wrong," and that may require considerable courage. It will also require responding knowledgeably and graciously when asked by another why one comes to the conclusion that one does, how one has reached a particular moral judgment.

It might also sound strange that anything so diverse and so complicated as ethical reflection can be talked about in terms of four major groups of methodological options. Of course, the study of anything requires categorization. Biology would be impossible without some system of grouping various kinds of living things. Neither chemistry nor physics could exist without some equivalent of the periodic table of elements. Historians need to come to some tentative agreements on date parameters for the Renaissance, or the advent of Modernity. Yet it seems strange to some that thinking about morality, which is so close to the marrow and fiber of human existence, can be categorized in such a seemingly simple way.

It may be resisted even by some who have labored in the field of ethics, some who have carved out for themselves a specific point of view that they want others to take seriously as a discreet option. It is understandable, for example, that a person who produces a given method and labels it "liberation ethics" may be reluctant to say that it is actually a form of teleology, or one who writes on "feminist ethics" that it is a variation of situationism. This is not to say that all "liberation ethics" positions are teleological, or that all "feminist ethics" positions are situational. The claim is rather that the four groups of methodological options to be discussed here do serve as a way of sorting out a wide variety of recommendations for doing ethics.

The amazing fact is that there is broad agreement among ethicists on major groupings of ethical methods. There have been many attempts to classify theological methods in various ways. These attempts are interesting and helpful, but no general agreement exists among theologians about what the groupings and their designations should be. In ethics the situation is quite different. It is possible to say that there are four generally acknowledged major methodological groupings: deontology, situationism, teleology, and character ethics.

Not every writer in ethics lists these options in exactly the same way. Sometimes one finds only deontology and teleology contrasted as the two great opposing systems. Sometimes different terms will be used. Situationism is called contextualism, personalism, relational ethics, act-deontology, or act-utilitarianism by different writers. Character ethics is often referred to as virtue ethics. We shall comment on these various terms as we look at each of the four groups.

Other descriptive and qualifying comments will be made along the way. For example, deontology, situationism, and teleology concentrate on the act, the decision, the deed. Character ethics concentrates on the actor, the person who performs the act, makes the decision, does the deed. It is a major shift and a very different way of thinking about the moral life.

It is also true, of course, that a method need not reject any interest whatever in an emphasis of another. Teleology, for example, pays attention to the situation at hand, but that does not make it situationism. It is also important to note that these methods are not vending machines. They do not produce automatic answers to moral questions. Two deontologists may come to opposite conclusions on a given issue or case. A deontologist and a teleologist may come to the same conclusion on a given issue or case, even though they may arrive at their conclusion in very different ways. The method is not itself a conclusion, but a way of thinking through an issue or a case toward a conclusion. All of these and more descriptive and qualifying matters will be dealt with as we examine these four major groupings.

An attempt has been made to present these options sympathetically. The reader is requested to approach each method with the possibility that it might sound attractive as a way to do ethics. Each is a legitimate option, or it would not be considered. Each is a possible way for Christians to do ethics, or it would not be included in a book about Christian Ethics. It is hoped that the reader will engage each description, but will also suspend final judgment until all four options have been described.

11. Deontology and Universal Moral Obligations

So act that you can will your action as a universal law for all humankind.
—Immanuel Kant

Deontological methods distinguish moral from non-moral judgments and work with moral obligations considered to be universally applicable.

The third section of this book will elaborate a consequentialist method of doing ethics in the context of Christian commitments, and it will be stated that this is a form of teleology, one of the four methodological groupings now being discussed. Although the first two sections of this book aim to be primarily descriptive, it has been acknowledged that the author's own position inevitably feeds back into the descriptive work. One example of this is that in talking about the institution of morality, the term "degree of moral density" was offered as an alternative to the sharp distinction between the moral and the non-moral. In this chapter we shall examine deontology, a method of doing ethics that does make a sharp distinction between the moral and the non-moral and that treats these two in very different ways. Although deontology is not the position of the author, it is clearly an important methodological option that should be given very serious consideration by anyone interested in the doing of ethics.

Deontology is probably the most common understanding of morality and the most commonly used method of doing ethics, whether or not those who embrace it have ever heard the term. Simply stated, people who work with deontological methods believe that some things are always and everywhere morally wrong, and some things are always and everywhere morally right. Morality as such is defined in terms of universal obligation. It is contrasted to matters thought to be non-moral, matters that are not governed by universal obligation, but rather by prudent decisions thought to be made, in part at least, out of self-interest. Deontologists believe that every reasonable person should be able, for example, to agree that things such as telling the truth and keeping promises are moral matters, and that obligations in these matters apply to every person in every time and in every place.

Deontologists specifically reject the teleological idea that the right should be done in order to bring about some good result. If good comes, it is a coincidence rather than a projected outcome. The right should be done for its own sake, simply because it is the right thing to do. In an illustration from Frankena to which we have previously made reference, leading a good life is a moral obligation that cannot be grounded in any expectation that it may result in having a good life, or even in a probability that many might have a better life than otherwise would be anticipated.

Deontology has a long and distinguished history that continues strong into the present time. Among important recent advocates are the philosopher John Rawls and the theologian Paul Ramsey. The person who gave it classic expression, and with whose name it is almost always associated, is Immanuel Kant, the great philosopher of the German Enlightenment. And, as Alasdair MacIntyre says in his *A Short History of Ethics,* for most people ethics is roughly what Kant said it is.[1] Kant did not invent deontology. He put into words what a great many people before and after him have thought and continue to think about morality and about ethics, whether they have ever heard of Immanuel Kant or thought about methods of ethical reflection.

The word "deontology" comes from the Greek verb *dei,* which means "it is necessary." Deontology is a way of thinking about morality that says that it is necessary to do some things and to avoid doing other things. Thus deontology is sometimes referred to as an ethic of necessity. It is at times called an ethic of duty. If it is necessary to do something, then it is my duty to do it. Although widely used in reference to deontology, the word "duty" is not very helpful because it is not sufficiently specific. Teleologists and situationists, for example, would also say that once a moral decision has been reached, it is one's duty to act on it.

The word "absolute" is often used to refer to a deontological way of understanding morality and of doing ethics. Deontologists deal with obligations that are taken to be absolute or universal, that is, not relative to time or place. Deontologists, therefore, reject teleological and situational positions that they believe encourage "moral relativism."

Although they work with moral absolutes, deontologists do not refer to themselves as "moral absolutists," probably because this term seems to carry a pejorative connotation, to imply an unthinking and biased allegiance to an arbitrary code of conduct. One does not have to spend much time reading John Rawls or Paul Ramsey to see that such a characterization of deontology would be totally false.

Kant's basic position is readily available and clearly stated in a small work titled, *Fundamental Principles of the Metaphysic of Morals.*[2] He begins by saying that there is nothing that can be conceived of as good without qualification other than a good will. He clarifies this with a number of negative statements. The good cannot be happiness, because it must be admitted that there are many immoral people who seem to be quite happy. It cannot be moderation, because a calm and careful murderer is probably even worse than one who murders in a fit of passion. It cannot be usefulness, because the good is something that shines like a jewel in and of itself. Usefulness cannot add or detract from that splendor. Kant knew that he was specifically rejecting the ethics of Aristotle, who praised *eudaimonia,* often translated "happiness," as the primary good toward which morality points. Aristotle also praised moderation, saying that every virtue is the moderate mean between two extremes, and usefulness, holding that moral behavior must be good for something, some end or goal, some *telos.* Kant could not be more clear about the fact that he is opposing Aristotelian teleology.

Kant continues in this little volume to say that the good cannot be inclination. If I am inclined to be nice to people, if I do it naturally and spontaneously, if it is my nature to treat people graciously, that is wonderful. But it is not a moral act. It is simply something that I do because I enjoy doing it. A moral act must be an act of the will, responding to an obligation. Thus the mood of moral obligation is never the indicative, that which is, but rather the imperative, that which ought to be. And that imperative cannot be what Kant calls a "hypothetical imperative," of the form, "If I do A, then B will occur." That would make usefulness a mark of the moral. The moral obligation must be a "categorical imperative," an imperative that calls for obedience totally without regard for the outcome. The good must be done for its own sake, because it is the right thing to do and for no other reason.

Kant then articulates a number of ways in which the categorical imperative can be expressed. One way is sometimes called "the formula of universal law." It reads, "So act that you can will your action as a universal law for all humankind." In other words, universalizability is the test to which one puts an act to determine whether it is truly a moral act. The formula is a sophisticated and carefully worded version of what many parents ask their child when some unacceptable behavior has been observed, namely, "What if everybody did that?" Kant believes that lying, for example, is always and everywhere morally wrong because he believes that no rational person is capable of universalizing lying, that is, of willing that everyone lie. Therefore, if you don't want everyone to do it, don't do it yourself. He argues similarly about suicide, neglecting charity, and misusing one's talents. These are only illustrations. The method is clear, and it is applicable across the entire spectrum of life. Morality itself is defined by the test of universalizability. If I am a rational person and I cannot will my action as a universal law for all humankind, it may still be an obligation for me, but it is not a moral obligation.

Another way Kant puts the categorical imperative is sometimes referred to as "the formula of the end-in-itself." It reads, "Never treat another human being merely as a means to an end, but always as an end-in-himself." Again, the argument is that no rational person is capable of universalizing the treating of people as means to some other end. Sisela Bok illustrates this by saying that everyone can at times rationalize lying as a quick way to avoid a given problem or embarrassment, but no rational person can universalize lying because nobody wants to be lied to.[3] Nobody wants to be used in this way toward the achievement of someone else's goal. The point is similar to Augustine's dictum that things are made to be used and people are made to be loved. It is therefore wrong to love things and to use people.

Deontology is a common understanding of morality and ethics that has been on the scene for a long time. Although the term itself was not used until the modern era, it can be argued that Plato and Socrates thought deontologically about morality, and that there are many places in the Bible that invite a deontological interpretation. One thinks immediately of the "Golden Rule," where Jesus says, "In everything do to others as you would have them do to you" (Matt.7:12).

One can find deontological arguments in Augustine and in Luther. In our own time, John Rawls' monumental work, *A Theory of Justice,* in which he argues for understanding justice as fairness, is done from a self-consciously deontological point of view.[4] He proposes that a person in what he calls "the original position," that is, unencumbered by personal experience and cultural influence, would say that people should be treated fairly. He believes that the moral view of justice is therefore egalitarian rather than meritarian, that fairness overrides every other idea of justice.[5] Another major philosopher who works with deontological commitments is Thomas Nagel, whose most recent book is titled *The Last Word.* He says, "Ideally, the aim is to arrive at principles that are universal and exceptionless. To reason is to think systematically in ways anyone looking over my shoulder ought to be able to recognize as correct."[6]

A superficial view of deontology may give the impression that it is a simplistic way of understanding morality and of doing ethics. Universal moral rules applicable to every person in every time and place may seem at first naive, unaware of life's complexities. It is important to say that deontologists are aware that universalizable rules for moral behavior may have to be carefully nuanced and written with meticulous attention to detail. Precisely because it is universally applicable, a deontological rule must be formulated in such a way that it can be applied to every relevant case. An example of a deontologist who worked with exquisite skill, attending with great care to every imaginable detail, is Paul Ramsey. His work in medical ethics, for example, in *The Patient as Person*[7] and in *Ethics at the Edges of Life,*[8] ought to demonstrate to any reader that deontology, when well done, is anything but simplistic.

If one is a Christian deontologist, one is probably going to take the Ten Commandments very seriously as moral rules. One is also probably going to believe that they were intended to convey the will of God for all people. If one takes, for example, "You shall not kill" as a universal moral rule, one's work as an ethicist may have just begun. The question of the meaning of the rule comes immediately forward. If it is going to apply to every person in every place and every time, it must be understood clearly and stated carefully.

No two deontologists would proceed with the same details in the same way, but all would proceed asking the same question, how to understand the prohibition of killing as a universal moral law. A specific Christian deontologist may use biblical and other sources to reach the conclusion that in order to be clear, one must understand the rule to mean, "You shall not kill another human being." This understanding, for example, would allow the killing of a carrot plant or even a chicken. A vegetarian deontologist could disagree and argue that the rule should read, "You shall not kill another human being or any other animal."

Or, to put it more specifically, there are Christian deontologists who believe that the commandment "You shall not kill" means that all killing of human beings, including killing that takes place in war and in self-defense, is always and everywhere wrong. Paul Ramsey was an example of a Christian deontologist who argued that war may, under certain conditions, be justified, as may the taking of another human life under conditions where one's own life is unmistakably being threatened by lethal force.[9] He argued against capital punishment and for the humane treatment of prisoners of war on the ground that taking another human life when that person poses no threat to one's own life or to that of another can never, under any circumstances, be justified. A deontological rule about not killing may have details built into the rule, but once it is thought to be clear, the rule, along with the built-in details, becomes universally applicable. A Christian deontologist who proceeds in this way does not consider the process as one of qualifying the original commandment, but rather as understanding it clearly and stating it carefully.

There are deontologists, both Christian and not Christian, who argue that it is a universal moral law that a woman's reproductive freedoms must never be violated. There are deontologists, both Christian and not Christian, who argue that it is a universal moral law that the life of an unborn child should never be deliberately destroyed. There are also, among deontologists, many refinements of these positions. As is the case with other methodological options, the method does not deliver automatic conclusions and should never be confused with any conclusion to which a particular deontologist comes. The method is not a conclusion to a moral question, but a way of understanding morality and of going about the task of doing ethics toward the reaching of a conclusion.

There is nothing simplistic about deontology when it is carefully done. Life may be seen as extremely complex. Moral rules, because they must be applicable to everyone in situations that are similar in morally relevant ways, have to be formulated with great care. Deontologists may come to very different conclusions on the same question, but they will work in the same way. What unifies deontologists is the conviction that moral issues do exist and that they need to be treated differently from non-moral matters. When dealing with morality, we are dealing with things that are right or wrong, rather than merely wise or foolish, beneficial or detrimental, pleasing or displeasing, useful or not useful. And the test for a truly moral rule is the test of universalizability.

Every group of ethical methodologies has its own innate problems. If deontology is not done with great care, the moral rules that it produces can become legalistic. That is, they may be forced to apply to situations in which they do not fit and so may be seen to be applied in arbitrary ways. But deontology is probably no more prone to legalism than is any other group of methods.

A problem that sometimes arises is what can be called a conflict of duties. One may promise, for example, not to divulge a particular piece of information about a friend. When then one is asked directly about it, it may be difficult to keep the promise and also to tell the truth. Any serious deontologist working with universal moral rules must figure out some way to deal with these conflict-of-duty situations. One such deontologist was the British philosopher W. D. Ross, who talked about both *prima facie* duties, that is, duties that are obligatory in principle, and *actual* duties, that is, duties that may in fact be obligatory due to factors not anticipated in the rule as formulated.[10] In his system, *actual* duties were thought to override *prima facie* duties when the two come into conflict. One could perhaps argue that Ross has abandoned deontology for situationism. A more likely analysis is that Ross has slightly modified Kantian deontology to accommodate those situations that present a difficult conflict of duties.

There are ethicists who talk about act-deontology as well as rule-deontology. The position taken here is that it is an unhelpful distinction. When used, the only thing that ties the two together is that in each case, the appeal is to the will to do its duty, whether that means one particular necessary act or the following of a universal rule. As has been said earlier in this chapter, however, all ethical positions deal with things that are considered duties to be done, so duty has no specific connection to deontology. The author believes that the term "deontology" should be reserved for rule-deontology where the fundamental test of a moral rule is its universalizability. What some call act-deontology can, in the author's opinion, be better handled as a way to talk about ethical situationism.

12. Situationism and Appropriate Actions

... Do not look around yourself into universal history, you must look into your own personal history. Always in your present lies the meaning in history, and you cannot see it as a spectator, but only in your responsible decisions. In every moment slumbers the possibility of being the eschatological moment. You must awaken it.
        —*Rudolf Bultmann,* History and Eschatology

Situationist methods reject the possibility of universal moral rules and seek in every situation to determine what is the most appropriate thing to do.

—————

Situationism is so different from deontology that the two methods can be thought about as exact opposites. Situationism denies what deontology affirms and affirms what deontology denies. Situationists tend to think of deontology as moral absolutism, and deontologists tend to think of situationism as moral relativism.

Situationism is a method of doing ethics that has a long history and capable contemporary advocates among professional ethicists as well as among people who may know little about the discipline of ethics but are eager to lead moral lives. For some, situationism seems so obvious that it needs no argument or even explanation. For others, situationism is an invitation to abandon morality and to do whatever one feels like doing. Reasonable people of goodwill, including Christians, disagree not only about conclusions to moral questions, but also about how to reach those conclusions, and even about the nature of morality itself.

Whereas deontology says that in moral matters everything depends on whether or not the rule for action can be universalized, situationism says that in moral matters everything depends on the particulars of the situation in which the action takes place. The conviction is that situations differ from one another so radically that there is no possibility of a moral rule that applies universally. Situationism says that what is right in one situation may be wrong in another. It even considers the words "right" and "wrong" misleading in moral matters and prefers to talk about actions that are "appropriate" or "fitting" for the situation being considered. Morality is not about following rules that apply to all situations but about doing what is appropriate in whatever situation one finds oneself.

Because in the case of situationism everything depends on the situation, and because situations are thought to differ—sometimes radically—from one another, precise definitions of situationism are more difficult to formulate than are definitions of deontology. Some would even say that it is intrinsic to situationism that it defies any general definition, that to define it would be to destroy it. Only the details of the situation can feed into the determination of the appropriate action. To try to get at a general definition of situationism may be taken to be a complete missing of the point that situationism wants to make.

Nevertheless, situationism is a distinct cluster of ethical methodologies that requires serious consideration, and we have already begun to work at a general definition and description. It may be, however, that the best way to get an idea of what situationism is about is to look at a time when situationism was perhaps most clearly articulated and most persuasively advocated. That period of time was particularly evident during what is generally referred to as "the 60s" of the twentieth century, although the period began early in the twentieth century and still continues.

When many people hear the term "situation ethics," they think immediately of Joseph Fletcher. He published a book with that title in 1966.[1] It was the centerpiece in an energetic debate, not only in the United States, but in many other places throughout the world. During this period many books were published with some reference to situation ethics in the title. Articles in popular magazines and newspapers as well as in professional journals were published and widely discussed. During this period, Harvey Cox published *The Situation Ethics Debate*,[2] which gathered together a large number of statements from a wide range of people with varying opinions about this cultural phenomenon. During the 60s, it was difficult to imagine anyone even slightly alert who had not heard about situation ethics.

Variations on similar themes appeared under different designations. John A. T. Robinson published *Honest to God*,[3] which was translated into many languages and caused a worldwide stir. It was a piece of popular theology, a huge canvas painted with a very broad brush, and it attacked what was considered to be a pre-Copernican notion of a God who resides "out there," above all material and temporal life, a God who is defined in terms of changelessness. Robinson used three theologians, Paul Tillich, Rudolf Bultmann, and Dietrich Bonhoeffer, to make his point, even though these three are in many important respects significantly different from one another. His chapter on ethics is titled "The New Morality," but it is remarkably similar to the position described by Joseph Fletcher in *Situation Ethics*. The emphasis is on changing situations that require changing moral decisions.

To those who called his position a veiled justification of "the old immorality," Robinson insisted that the word "new" referred to the ethics of the New Testament, specifically the ethics of Jesus. He argued that the Good News of the New Testament required also a new morality that was dependent not on changeless universal rules but rather on openness to the new demands of new situations. Robinson used biblical and theological supports to spell out his conviction that "God is in the rapids as much as in the rocks, and as Christians we are free to swim and not merely to cling."[4] At about the same time, Bob Dylan was singing, "You better start swimmin' or you'll sink like a stone, for the times they are a changin'."[5]

Harvey Cox published a book during the same period with the title *The Secular City*.[6] It is a remarkable *tour de force,* ranging widely through cultural and theological landscapes with abundant references to biblical materials. He celebrates another major theme of the 60s, that of secularity, and argues that attention to the secular is a result of the proclamation of the Good News that God is not known by God's distance from the world, the secular, but rather by God's identification with it.

These themes had been around for a long time—some would insist since the inception of Christianity. There had been an emphasis on God active in history during years preceding "the situation ethics debate." For example, *The Book of the Acts of God* by G. Ernest Wright and Reginald Fuller was a widely used text.[7] The book referred to in the title is, of course, the Bible, and the point was that the Bible does not describe a God outside of time but rather a God who acts in history and time and change. Wright and Fuller's book was part of a larger movement that spread over several decades, sometimes referred to as the *Heilsgeschichte* or Holy History movement, sometimes as the Biblical Theology movement.

During the same period, Dorothy L. Sayers, the British writer of the Lord Peter Wimsey mystery stories, wrote a series of radio plays for the BBC on the life of Jesus, *The Man Born to be King.* One of the memorable lines in her introduction is, "There have been incarnate gods a-plenty, and slain and resurrected gods not a few; but He is the only God who has a date in history."[8] This is not to say that these trends in biblical interpretation were part of the Situation Ethics movement, only that they were compatible impulses.

Cox's book had everything to do with ethics and situationism. In a striking passage, he states that the world in which God acts is like a floating craps game in which the task of the Christian is to ask, "Where's the action?" and to get in on that action, namely, on what God is now doing in the world.[9] That is, the task is not to do the thing that is always and everywhere right, but to get so inside a situation that one can sense what needs doing in this here and in this now. For Cox, the point was that God is located precisely in our midst, in our time and place, and this fact makes it possible for Christians to embrace this secular city rather than some timeless and changeless distant place. For those who know Augustine's *The City of God,* the radical shift is obvious. Cox's book gave rise to a volume of essays, as had Fletcher's, and was similarly titled *The Secular City Debate.*[10] It should not be surprising that there was also a volume of essays titled *The Honest to God Debate.*[11]

These three books by Fletcher, Robinson, and Cox were translated into many languages and sold many thousands of copies worldwide because they picked up and articulated a theme that struck a chord with vast numbers of people. That theme was the importance of this moment with its opportunities and challenges, rather than the past or the future time or the distant place. All three authors were Christians, and all were passionately committed to expressing clearly what they believed Christian faith and life to be about.

The situationism of the 60s did not spring into being out of nothing. It is of a piece with other large cultural movements of the middle decades of the twentieth century. Movements having to do with biblical interpretation have already been mentioned. A philosophical movement extremely congenial to ethical situationism was existentialism. Although the philosopher most closely associated with the origins of this movement, Søren Kierkegaard, worked in Denmark a century earlier, existentialism as a broad philosophical and cultural movement did not take hold until after World War I, and it did not fully bloom until after World War II.

The setting was a world torn apart and disillusioned. The nineteenth century had been "a century of progress" in the development of industry and communication. It had been accompanied by a worldview that had believed in progress as inevitable. It had been a time of great optimism in which everything seemed possible, if only sufficient education and energy could be brought to bear on whatever problem needed solving. After World War I, these hopes were at least temporarily smashed, and all that mattered seemed to be the present moment in which perhaps some meaning could be found. The focus was not on the distant past nor on an uncertain future, but on the present situation. The time was ripe for existentialism, a movement that was explicit about the supreme importance of the moment at hand.

The demise of optimism brought about by the devastation of world war, and the resultant move toward the immediate situation, the concrete event, the specific moment, was captured beautifully by Ernest Hemingway in words he places into the mouth of a returning soldier in the novel A Farewell to Arms.

> I was always embarrassed by the words sacred, glorious, and sacrifice and the expression in vain. We had heard them, sometimes standing in the rain, almost out of earshot, so that only the shouted words came through, and had read them, on proclamations that were slapped up by billposters over other proclamations now for a long time, and I had seen nothing sacred, and the things that were glorious had no glory, and the sacrifices were like the stockyards at Chicago if nothing was done with the meat except to bury it. There were many words that you could not stand to hear and finally only the names of places had dignity. Certain numbers were the same way and certain dates and these with the names of places were all you could say and have them mean anything. Abstract words such as glory, honor, courage, or hallow were obscene beside the concrete names of villages, the numbers of roads, the names of rivers, the numbers of regiments and the dates.[12]

The movement found expression among some with no Christian commitments, such as Jean-Paul Sartre and Simone de Beauvoir in France.[13] De Beauvoir wrote *The Ethics of Ambiguity,* an existentialist treatment of ethics. The time is World War II, but some of the lines are remarkably similar to those words of Hemingway's returning soldier. De Beauvoir writes:

> I remember having experienced a great feeling of calm on reading Hegel in the impersonal framework of the Bibliothèque Nationale in August 1940. But once I got out into the street again, into my life, out of the system, beneath a real sky, the system was no longer of any use to me: what it had offered me, under a show of the infinite, was the consolations of death; and I again wanted to live in the midst of living men.[14]

There were also Christian theologians such as the early Karl Barth in Switzerland and later Rudolf Bultmann at the University of Marburg in Germany. Bultmann was very clear about his commitments to existentialism, which are evident throughout his entire theological work. Thomas C. Oden captures the heart of Bultmann's ethics in his comment:

> The elusive question we have been pursuing is, "What does the moment demand?" Bultmann stakes his whole answer to this question on the command to love God and to love one's neighbor as oneself. *Although the command is a formal statement of what ought to be done, the actual deed of loving the neighbor is always the unique content of the calling of the moment.*[15]

No such monumental figures appeared in Great Britain or in the United States, where language philosophy, rather than existentialism, dominated the philosophical scene as a reaction to nineteenth-century idealism. Yet existentialism was a widely pervasive movement, affecting art, literature, and drama as well as philosophy, theology, and ethics. For a time, philosophical and theological existentialism and ethical situationism were so pervasive that it was difficult to entertain the possibility that there were other options.

Deontologists believe that morality has to do with universal moral obligations and therefore work to find or to formulate universalizable moral rules. Situationists believe that morality has to do with obligations demanded by particular situations and therefore work to get inside situations, to describe those situations accurately, and to allow the decision to emerge from the concrete details of that situation. They are fond of using stories to illustrate how the method works. The stories become paradigmatic, or illustrative, for the method.

Jean-Paul Sartre, for example, tells about a young man living in Paris during the German occupation in World War II.[16] He has an obligation to stay at home and take care of his ailing mother. He also has an obligation to join the Free French and fight for the liberation of his country. Sartre details the situation and leaves it there. The point is that nobody can tell the young man what is the right thing to do. There are no universal moral rules that can sort things out for him. In the midst of the ambiguity, he must make a decision based on his best sense about the total situation. The only "wrong" thing for him to do would be to refuse to face the situation squarely, to allow by default external events to make the decision for him. His moral obligation is to "exist," to grasp reality in the midst of the ambiguity.

An illustration of another situationist story is found in a book by the Lutheran theologian Joseph Sittler, *The Structure of Christian Ethics*.[17] The story is taken from a novel, *The Cruel Sea*. During an Allied convoy trip across the Atlantic to Europe in World War II, a German submarine sinks one of the ships in the convoy. Survivors are floating on the surface in life jackets among the debris and oil slick. The captain of a destroyer zeros in on the submarine with his sonar device. At this point he has to make a decision. He can throw depth charges and get the submarine, but in doing so he will also endanger his own people in the life jackets. Or he can pick up the survivors, refrain from using the depth charges, and allow the submarine to go on, perhaps to sink more Allied ships. The captain stands on the deck of the destroyer, looks out into the darkness, and says, "One must do what one must do—and say one's prayers." Again, there is no "right" thing to do, nor is there a universal moral rule to follow. A decision must be made in the midst of the ambiguities of the situation.

Christian situationists are attracted to stories in the Bible, particularly to the parables of Jesus, who seems often to have told stories in response to questions. The story of the Good Samaritan is a classic illustration. The people who pass by on the other side are people who apparently think about it and decide they have important things to do that cannot be delayed. The Good Samaritan sees a person in need and immediately responds to what the situation demands, presumably without deeply pondering the options. Christian situationists like to point to the remark of Jesus that all of the Law and the prophets are summed up in love to God and love to neighbor. Love is always demanded, but the specifics of how that demand is fulfilled cannot be prescribed by rules. That all depends on the situation. (It should be said, parenthetically, that not only situationists focus on love. Paul Ramsey, a prime example of a Christian deontologist, focused on love, but in a very different way. He believed that agape-embodying rules could be formulated that encoded universal moral obligations.)

There are many ways in which situation ethics is talked about. We have already mentioned the term "The New Morality." We have discussed existentialism and suggested that all philosophical existentialists are ethical situationists. "Existentialist ethics," therefore, is a term closely related to situation ethics. Sometimes the term "contextualism" is used, as in Paul Lehmann's *Ethics in a Christian Context*.[18] That term is usually employed to indicate that the situation is not necessarily a narrow one involving only a few people. The situation may be a broader context with concentric circles of involved people. For this reason Lehmann also refers to his position as a *koinonia* ethic. Because he emphasizes God's initiative, he says that the primary ethical question is, "What is God doing to make and to keep human life human?" The moral task of the Christian is to "get in on" that activity of God.[19]

Ethicists who talk about "act-deontology" and "act-utilitarianism" are in fact describing what we are calling here "situationism." In each case, morality and ethical reflection have to do with single actions, not universal or even general rules. The same is true of so-called divine-command theory, a term that is sometimes used to point to a single act commanded by God, an act that follows no rules and cannot be transferred to other situations. The command of God to Abraham to kill his son Isaac is an example. Robin Gill uses the term "personalism" for describing a situationist ethic. Various forms of "relational ethics," as in H. Richard Niebuhr's *The Responsible Self*, are essentially situational methods of doing ethics.[20] It is also the case that some interpretations of Martin Luther and of the apostle Paul, which emphasize living in the full freedom of the gospel instead of living under the bondage of the law, are in fact radically situationist ethical methodologies. There is no question that there are passages in Luther's writings and also in the Pauline letters to which one can point to make a persuasive argument in this direction. It would be a mistake to make a simple claim that Luther and Paul are situationists, but it is understandable that the materials are there to build such a case.

An obvious danger in deontology is that it can degenerate into legalism. An obvious danger in situationism is that it can degenerate into libertinism (antinomianism). Some situationists attempt to curb this possibility by expanding the raw situation into a broader context, or a wider set of relationships. Others allow for "rules of thumb," or "presumptive rules," or "cumulative rules," all of which are taken to be useful but never universal or absolute.

It is easy to see how anyone dissatisfied with deontology and universal moral obligations might be attracted to ethical situationism with its focus on appropriate actions. Situationism is, however, not the only alternative to deontology. We have yet to look at teleology and character ethics.

13. Teleology and the Common Good

So we say that a ship is under control when it is sailed on the right course to port by the skill of a sailor. Now when something is ordered to an end which lies outside itself, as a ship is to harbour, it is the ruler's duty not only to preserve its integrity, but also to see that it reaches its appointed destination.
—*Thomas Aquinas*, On Princely Government

Teleological methods understand morality as having to do with actions thought to have high degrees of probability to bring about outcomes that will increase the common good and decrease human ills.

We have seen that deontology and situationism can be understood as polar opposites. What one affirms the other rejects. It would be possible to argue that teleology can be located somewhere between these two, that there are both similarities and differences between it and each of the other two methodological options thus far discussed. For example, it could be said that teleology resembles deontology in that it is willing to formulate rules for moral behavior, and it resembles situationism in that it is committed to incorporating observed data from actual situations into the moral equation and the doing of ethics. On the other hand, one could say that teleology differs from deontology in that it specifically rejects the deontological requirement to "do the right thing" without any regard for consequences, and differs from situationism in that it insists on stretching out the moral time line from the present into short- and long-term projections of probable future outcomes.

The position taken here is that it is more helpful to understand teleology, not as located between deontology and situationism, but rather as a robust alternative to either of the other two, differing significantly from both and bearing its own unique characteristics. Every careful deontologist and every careful situationist know that teleology does not describe who they are, how they understand morality, or how they do ethics. The claim that teleology is somewhere between these two, the implication that it embraces the best of both and avoids problems in each, would correctly be seen as an arrogant move on the part of the author, who favors teleology. It is clearer and more accurate to treat teleology as a third methodological option.

The sharp distinction between deontology and teleology is well established and commonly described in ethics texts. Frankena, for example, states that teleological systems reject what deontological systems affirm, and vice versa.[1] In his section on classical ethical theories, Beauchamp treats these two (along with a third, character ethics) as "Mill and Utilitarian Theories" and "Kant and Deontological Theories."[2] Utilitarianism is a form of teleology. When talking about method, Robin Gill deals with deontology and consequentialism (along with a third, "personalism," his term for situationism).[3] Consequentialism is a form of teleology. The sharp distinction between deontology and teleology appears in literature and film, sometimes with two antagonists, each clearly representing one of these two points of view.

This sharp distinction can be expressed in many ways. In deontology, everything depends on doing the right thing, regardless of consequences, which, in any case, cannot be accurately anticipated. In teleology, everything depends on getting something good accomplished, even though one must work with probabilities rather than certainties. In deontology, the right thing to do is determined by its congruence with what are deemed to be universal moral obligations. It should be done because it is the right thing to do. In teleology, the good thing to do is determined by its likelihood to bring about results that will be beneficial for the common good. It should be done because of the good it will likely bring about.

The sharp contrast between situationism and teleology is not so explicit in some ethics texts. Beauchamp, for example, does not include situationism as a separate category in his section on ethical methods, although he deals with the other three that we are discussing.[4] As we have already observed, however, what we consider to be a distinct method that deserves its own description and evaluation is, in fact, discussed in most texts under a cluster of other terms, such as "act-deontology," "act-utilitarianism," "divine command theory." It may also be treated as a separate method, but given a different name, such as "personalism," "contextualism," or "relational ethics."

Another possible reason that the sharp distinction between situationism and teleology is sometimes not specified is that, from the

viewpoint of deontology, they look similar in their radical rejection
of deontology. From that perspective, the two seem to move in and
out of one another. Both reject the notion of universal moral obligations. Both can be attacked by deontology as promoting "moral relativism." Both insist that what *is* the case has something significant
to say about the formulation of what *ought* to be done. Both insist on
acknowledging considerable ambiguity in the moral landscape.
Despite these similarities as seen from the perspective of deontology,
the differences between situationism and teleology are striking and
decisive.

One massive distinction has to do with understandings of time.
Situationism has an episodic understanding of time. Meaning is
found in the moment, one of which follows another with no discernible connections. There are lightning flashes that illuminate for
a brief moment everything, but then there is total darkness, and
there is no way of knowing when or where the next flash will be. Situationism favors *kairos* over *chronos,* "significant time" over "chronological time." In Bultmann's distinction, drawing on nuances in the
German words for time, it favors *Geschichte* over *Historie.*

Teleology has an entirely different understanding of time, one
that is linear and chronological. It insists that *kairos* makes sense
only inside of *chronos,* and that *Geschichte* makes sense only inside of
Historie. Teleology believes that the kairotic dots can and must be
joined to one another in a continuous chronological timeline. Situationism flatly rejects this notion.[5] Teleology focuses on the future
goal. Thus time, for teleology, is not only linear, but directional,
always in motion toward the future. The moral act, therefore, is one
that projects into the future some good for human beings and for the
whole creation to which human beings are inextricably tied.

Situationism and teleology also have differing understandings of
God. If representatives of these positions are Christians, they find
themselves describing the God of the Bible in different ways. Situationism emphasizes the spontaneous and surprising characteristics of
God's intrusions into otherwise placid and predictable situations.
Teleology emphasizes the faithfulness of the covenant God, whose
surprises are always within the context of the keeping of covenant
promises. Reliability rather than spontaneity, faithfulness rather
than surprise, characterize God for Christian teleologists. Teleology

is a discrete option for doing ethics, in no way to be confused with either deontology or situationism.

The word "teleology" is derived from the Greek word *telos,* which means "end" or "goal." Teleological methods say that everything depends on the projected end results of the action, on the proposed consequences of the behavior. According to these methods, the only way to make a sound decision is to ask about probable outcomes of various alternatives for action. One should then do that which one concludes will probably bring about the most good for the greatest number of people and the least harm. Both deontology and situationism reject this fundamental commitment of teleology.

A useful definition of teleology can be found in Frankena. He says, with great care, that a teleological theory states ". . . an act is *right* if and only if it or the rule under which it falls produces, will probably produce, or is intended to produce *at least as great a balance of good over evil* as any available alternative."[6] It is a useful definition because it contains the ingredients that are important to any clear understanding of the position. One way to get inside teleology is to look at these ingredients.

Teleology abandons any claim to moral certainty. Teleologists work with probable futures and know that things often turn out differently from how one thinks they will. They know that this happens with sufficient frequency to warrant the formulation of what some call "The Law of Unintended Consequences." They know that the future cannot be predicted with accuracy. They know that what they project as a good outcome may turn out very badly. Yet they are not likely to join those who declare that "the road to Hell is paved with good intentions." In the vocabulary of teleology, an "intention" is not an empty or casual desire, but rather a conscious decision that moves in a chosen direction after careful analysis of available options.

Teleologists recognize that it would be nice to live with greater certainty about something as important as morality, yet they think there is nowhere else to go and no other way to understand the real world. They think that getting something good accomplished is what morality is about, and that there is therefore no live alternative to making the best projections one can and then acting on that information. Feedback devices must be built into the process, so that mid-course corrections can be made along the way. It is essential to monitor the progress once something is set in motion so that these adjustments can be made. A conscious attempt to avoid irreversible mistakes is essential, even though such errors will certainly occur from time to time.

The presuppositions and procedures are similar to, some might say identical to, ways in which prudent people live their lives and make important decisions in many other areas of life. Probability, rather than certainty, is what living in the real world is about. Degrees of probability vary widely, but absolute certainty does not exist, unless one wants to say it exists in the minds of some individuals. But it does not exist in the world outside of ourselves, not even in the hard sciences, certainly not in personal relationships or even in matters of faith. Morality is a fluid and porous social institution. The teleologist wonders why anyone should think it strange that it should deal with probabilities rather than certainties.

The projected goal is never a pure good, but the greatest balance of good over evil that is possible considering available options. This is due not only to the difficulty of projecting outcomes, but to the fact that no pure good exists in this world. This argument can be made on secular grounds by referring, for example, to the ambiguity of situations and the frailty of human beings. But in this text having to do with Christian Ethics, it is enough to point to the Christian doctrine of sin, which says that everything in this creation is distorted, out of joint, in need of redemption. Paul talks about the whole creation being in bondage to decay (Rom. 8:21). In this existence permeated by sin, the greatest balance of good over evil is as good as it gets. The Christian theologian and social critic Reinhold Niebuhr, who reflected a great deal on the reality of sin, knew that "proximate justice" was not only a worthy goal, but the only possible goal for Christians realistically to pursue.

The teleologist knows that it is not possible to examine carefully all available options. One does what one can. Having already abandoned the quest for absolute certainty, aware that actions sometimes have unintended consequences, knowing that pure good does not exist in this world, the teleologist is free to look at as many options as possible, make an attempt to weigh probable risks and benefits, and then to act, monitoring as carefully as possible whatever happens, aware that mid-course corrections will probably need to be made. The teleologist believes that this is what we have to work with. It is what the real world is like. The human race has been able to accomplish a great deal under these conditions of uncertainty. There is good reason to be hopeful that good things can continue to happen, even though, as Christians say, there will be nothing but mixed goods until the last day.

Some ethicists speak about teleological systems being "egoistic." The assumption seems to be that if one acts prudently, one necessarily acts in one's own interest. The assumption is at best strange. Of course many people do behave in egoistic ways. But our powers of self-deception are such that it is possible to turn any ethical methodology into an egoistic system. Teleology as an understanding of morality and a way of doing ethics is intrinsically altruistic, as is each of the other three methodologies. The institution of morality would not exist apart from a fundamental commitment to altruism.

An example of teleology at work in our time is a fascinating new interest in "the common good" tradition.[7] It has deep roots in Aristotle but can be found in Augustine and abundantly in Thomas Aquinas. It is specifically spelled out in the Utilitarian movement, led by such figures as Jeremy Bentham and John Stuart Mill in eighteenth- and nineteenth-century England. Utilitarians worked to change laws so that child labor and debtors' prisons could be eliminated and were active in the struggle for women's suffrage. One of the ways they formulated their goals was "the greatest good for the greatest number." They attempted to check any tendency to increase the well-being of the majority at the expense of the minority by insisting that "each one counts for one and no one counts for more than one."[8]

The common good tradition finds its way into the United States Constitution in the guarantee of rights to "life, liberty, and the pursuit of happiness." American pragmatism, with its stress on the question whether something in fact "works" and moves effectively to get the job done, has affinities to the common good tradition and can be understood as a variant of teleological understandings of morality and ethics. *Commonweal* is a Roman Catholic journal that takes its name from this tradition.[9] After Robert Bellah and his group analyzed the fundamental problem of individualism in the United States in their book *Habits of the Heart*,[10] they did a second volume,

The Good Society.[11] Its response to the problem of individualism is that the social institutions in the United States need redeeming, but that they are redeemable. In that redemption lies our greatest hope for the development of the good society. It can be understood as a carrying on of the common good tradition.

The most obvious problem intrinsic to teleological thinking about morality and ethics is that those using this method must take care not to fall into the error of thinking that the pursuit of the good justifies any route to its achievement, that is, that "the end justifies the means." The antidote to this problem is the realization that both ends and means are multiple and complex, that long, mid-range, and short-term goals must be taken into consideration, and that projected outcomes must be regularly monitored so that mid-course corrections can be put into effect along the way. Means that are chosen must be commensurate with ends that are sought. Otherwise they will surely be counterproductive.

In Part 3 we shall attempt to spell out a consideration of consequentialism, a way of talking about teleology, as an option for doing Christian Ethics. Before we do that, we need to look at quite a different group of ethical methodologies, that of character or virtue ethics.

14. Character Ethics and the Virtues

In the same way, every good tree bears good fruit, but the bad tree bears bad fruit. A good tree cannot bear bad fruit, nor can a bad tree bear good fruit.
                                    —*Jesus in Matthew, 7:17f.*

Advocates of character ethics consider the emphasis on decisions and actions, maintained by deontology, situationism, and teleology, to be misplaced. They believe that morality should focus not on the act, but on the person who acts.

There is a gathered position in ethics known as character ethics or virtue ethics. It goes back at least as far as Aristotle, but as recently as the 1970s it was not formally included as a specific ethical position in many ethics texts. It has always been present as a way to think about morality, but there has not always been a specific group of ethicists working to articulate the position in a careful and persuasive way. At the present time, character ethics is a major option that nobody interested in the discipline of ethics can ignore. The following lead sentences in an article on character ethics, written in 1990 and even truer today, emphasize the recent growth in interest:

> A fashionable opening, for a time, to reviews of works on virtue was to note and often bemoan the neglect of the topic. That rhetorical gambit can no longer be used: indeed what only ten years ago was a cottage industry threatens to become an industrial giant.[1]

It would be almost impossible to confuse character ethics with any of the other three methodological options discussed here. This kind of ethics is a major shift in focus. Character ethicists argue that morality is not a matter having to do with universal moral obligations (deontology), or with appropriate deeds in specific situations (situationism), or with future goods to be worked for in the present (teleology). Morality, character ethicists say, does not find its focus in the act at all, but rather in the actor. The focus is on character rather than conduct, on being rather than behaving, on who one is rather than on what one does. Morality is a matter, one could say, of the heart. Morality has to do not so much with what appears on the outside of a person, but with what is on the inside.

It would be inaccurate, in this author's opinion, to describe Dietrich Bonhoeffer as a character ethicist, but he expresses a character ethics point of view when he states, "What is worse than doing evil is being evil. It is worse for a liar to tell the truth than for a lover of truth to lie."[2] The sentence is carefully crafted. He is not condoning the lie. He is expressing in a striking way the character ethics point of view that morality should focus on the person rather than on the act. The importance of being a teller of the truth is greater than that of a single act of telling a truth or a lie. It would take some doing to argue that Martin Luther was a character ethicist, but he expresses, in part at least, this understanding of morality when he says in "The Freedom of a Christian," "Good works do not make a good man, but a good man does good works; evil works do not make a wicked man, but a wicked man does evil works."[3] By highlighting different sayings of Jesus, one can argue that he was a proponent of any of the four methods described in this book. But he expresses the position of a character ethicist when he says, "In the same way, every good tree bears good fruit, but the bad tree bears bad fruit" (Matt. 7:17).

Christian character ethicists have no problem finding biblical support for their position. The wisdom literature is full of such references. "Happy are those who do not follow the advice of the wicked, or take the path that sinners tread, or sit in the seat of scoffers. . . . They are like trees planted by streams of water, which yield their fruit in its season, and their leaves do not wither. In all that they do, they prosper" (Ps. 1:1-3). "Train children in the right way, and when old, they will not stray" (Prov. 22:5). Jesus has already been quoted. Paul talks about the fruit of the Spirit and lists a recognizable series of virtues: love, joy, peace, patience, kindness, generosity, faithfulness, gentleness, and self-control (Gal. 5:22f). The author of Ephesians says to fasten the belt of truth and put on the breastplate of righteousness (Eph. 6:14).

Every character ethicist, whether embracing Christian commitments or not, knows that the position has deep roots in Aristotle. In *The Nicomachean Ethics*,[4] Aristotle says that the good is that at which all things point. It is a very different orientation from that of Kant, who says that it is impossible for anyone to conceive of anything that is good without qualification other than a good will. For Aristotle, everything has a proper end toward which it is directed, and the end toward which the human being is directed is the virtuous life. Life itself is a process of actualizing this potential. The virtuous life is one of *eudaimonia.* The term is often translated "happiness," but Aristotle knows that one good laugh does not constitute a life of *eudaimonia.* "For one swallow does not make a summer, nor does one day; and so too one day, or a short time, does not make a man blessed and happy." [5] When Aristotle talks about *eudaimonia,* he is talking about total well-being in which the whole self flourishes, including the total society in which that self is nourished. It must be noted that Aristotle did not move to eliminate the existing institution of slavery any more than did the apostle Paul. There are major differences between Aristotle and Paul on this matter, but that discussion is for another time and place.

According to Aristotle, one becomes a virtuous person by practicing the virtues. One becomes a truth-teller by practicing telling the truth. One becomes a promise-keeper by practicing keeping one's promises. Character is developed by the habituation of virtue. It is an entirely common-sense thing to say. Everyone knows that one becomes a piano player by practicing playing the piano, or a cello player by practicing playing the cello. Lewis B. Smedes tells about when Pablo Casals was ninety years old and was asked why he worked so hard, practicing playing his cello four or five hours a day. Casals replied, "Because I think I am making some progress." [6] One becomes a good driver by practicing good driving habits. One becomes a considerate person by practicing considerate behavior. Of course, we begin the process with different endowments, different DNA. But the process itself seems obvious. Why should not one become a virtuous person by practicing the virtues? Parents know that parenting involves precisely this, the building up in their children of the kind of good habits that will turn them into people with dispositions, attitudes, and traits that move them into a useful and gracious adulthood.

Aristotle spoke of four primary virtues: prudence, justice, courage, and temperance. But he detailed a great many more, including such things as pride, wit, and patience—each one described as "the golden mean" between two extremes. When the full texts of Aristotle reached the West, having been brought across North Africa with the movement of Islam, then across the Straits of Gibraltar into southern Spain and finally to Paris in the thirteenth century, Thomas Aquinas arrived there to study with the Dominican Albertus Magnus. Aquinas drank deeply at this Aristotelian well and developed a theology heavily dependent upon Aristotelian philosophy. Aquinas quotes Aristotle regularly, but rarely gives his name. He refers to him simply as "the philosopher."

To the four primary virtues of Aristotle, Aquinas adds the three "theological virtues" of faith, hope, and love. The ethical system was essentially the same. In Christian terms, for example, one became a loving person by habituating love, that is, by practicing the art of loving. For Aquinas, there could be no conflict between the philosophical and the theological virtues, since as grace always fulfills and never destroys nature, so the theological virtues always fulfill and never destroy the philosophical virtues.

This infuriated Martin Luther, who had a more radical understanding of human depravity, and thus a more radical understanding of the transformation that the grace of God brings about in the repentant sinner. Luther did not believe, any more than did Aquinas, that grace destroys nature. But he did believe that grace radically changes nature, rather than simply fulfilling it. Thus good works cannot make a person good and the practice of virtue cannot make a person virtuous. A person can only be made good by the saving grace of God, and even that goodness is not a moral goodness, but a righteousness declared by God on the basis of the finished redemptive work of Jesus Christ. The one who is declared righteous remains a sinner and continues to sin, for which daily repentance and daily renewal of the baptismal covenant is necessary.

So Aquinas and Aristotle are ready targets for Luther's volatile polemic, as is *habitus,* or the entire idea of the habituation of virtue. There are a number of recurring themes in Luther's work. The most consistent target is the legalism, or "works righteousness," which he saw in the Roman Catholic church of his day. Luther insisted that Christians were *simul iustus et peccator,* at the same time justified and sinner. Their justification is not because of their own good works, but because they are declared righteous on the basis of the finished redemptive work of God in Jesus Christ. Thus faith in Christ becomes the criterion for the Christian life. If one acts in faith, it is good. If one acts apart from faith, it is not.[7] This is a dominant and persistent theme, even though Luther's understanding of the Christian life is complex and not always consistent.

At first glance, it seems that anyone devoted to the theology of Luther cannot be an exponent of character ethics. And that makes it all the more interesting that one of the premier character ethicists of our time is Gilbert Meilaender, Board of Directors Professor of Theological Ethics at Valparaiso University. Meilaender is a Lutheran ethicist who works specifically with Lutheran commitments. He sees no problem in identifying himself as a character ethicist, and he is clear that he works with Luther and Aristotle at the same time.[8] The point is not whether character formation is possible. Every parent knows that it is and must be. The point is whether this is something that we take credit for or something for which we give thanks to God. Meilaender says that God works in people to bring them into the community of those who are justified even while sinners. This community, however, is the arena in which God works to help people become who they are, to actualize and practice in their behavior the kind of righteousness that has been bestowed upon them by grace through faith in Jesus Christ. One of Meilaender's major works is aptly titled *The Theory and Practice of Virtue*.[9] Another volume is dedicated to a study of a single virtue. The title is *Friendship*.[10]

Meilaender is one of a cluster of contemporary character ethicists, people who know that they work with this methodology and are explicit about it. Bernard Williams is looked to by many as a major source of the new beginnings of this position. Some date the current new explosion of interest in character ethics from the 1981 publication of Alasdair MacIntyre's work *After Virtue*.[11] Probably the most prolific writer among Christians doing character ethics is Stanley Hauerwas. His productivity is almost overwhelming and extends over a vast landscape of ideas and issues. The current literature in character ethics ranges from very popular works, such as the one by Lewis B. Smedes, mentioned above, *A Pretty Good Person*, to the very scholarly work of Jean Porter on Thomas Aquinas, *The Rediscovery of Virtue*.[12] Character ethics has also captured the imagination of Stephen L. Carter, professor at Harvard Law School. Two of his books are *Civility* and *Integrity*.[13] Sara Lawrence-Lightfoot, also at Harvard, has published *Respect: An Exploration*.[14]

The fact that character ethics is a cultural movement as well as a scholarly pursuit is evidenced, for example, in the widespread reception of two works by William J. Bennett, *The Book of Virtues*[15] and *The Moral Compass*.[16] Each chapter in *The Book of Virtues* has a single virtue for a title, such as self-discipline, compassion, responsibility, courage, perseverance, honesty, loyalty, faith, etc. In each chapter, there are stories, poems, and biographical pieces. There are no long or intricate explanations of each virtue. The idea is that one learns the virtue by exposure to the practice of the virtue by people in the story or the poem or the biographical piece. Consistent with this position, Bennett has also published *The Children's Book of Virtues*.[17] One of Stanley Hauerwas's favorite stories, which he draws from extensively, is *Watership Down*.[18]

If one were to risk a massive oversimplification, it could be said that the virtues are "caught" rather than "taught." The comment is not entirely frivolous. Aristotle thought that the "intellectual virtues" could be taught but the "moral virtues" could be developed only by habituation. Character development takes time. It is necessary to live in a family that is part of a community in which values are shared and virtues are practiced, histories are remembered, stories are told, narratives are constructed and repeated. One learns to be an honest person not only by practicing honesty, but by observing honest people who also tell stories about people who are honest even when it demands great sacrifice and courage. Christian character ethicists are quick to point out that society in general cannot be the primary arena for the development of character. Christians must exist as "resident aliens"[19] in a world to which they do not owe their first allegiance.

Some criticize this "little flock" mentality and believe that there is something intrinsically sectarian about character ethics in a Christian context. Christians who want to emphasize that Christian people should be in the world and for the world, even though not "of" the world, tend to see the themes of character ethics leading to a withdrawal from society. They may even think that it leads automatically to a "Christ against culture" stance, to use a phrase from H. Richard Niebuhr.[20]

It is true that there is a strong emphasis on cohesive communities with strong commitments and shared narratives, but advocates have abundant resources to which to point, both in the Bible and in the Christian tradition, to support their claims. The life of Jesus and the small group of early followers is interpreted in this way. It was by witnessing this radical new style of life being modeled before their eyes that the world began to turn to the Christian way. Christianity is not something to argue. It is something to live.

It would be difficult to find anyone who is against developing people of good character who live virtuous lives. It is obvious that without some good character traits, without some inner drive to lead a good life, all of the combined ethical reflection in the world is worthless. Some degree of virtue, some kind of character strength, is a prerequisite even for an interest in morality. Character ethics says more than this. It claims not only that character and virtue ought to be worked for and encouraged, but that this is what morality is about. The claim is specifically that a focus on moral acts is misplaced, and that if virtuous people of good character are nurtured and encouraged, the actions will take care of themselves.

There are problems, as there are with every group of methods. The possibility of withdrawing into a sectarian little flock of good people has already been mentioned. Perhaps the greatest problem, however, is the lack of mechanisms for adjudicating differences in moral judgment. If the entire focus is on the character, the virtuous inclinations, the laudable dispositions of the actor, how does one enter into conversation when two people of virtuous character disagree on an important moral choice, issue, or case?

If two Christians are delegates to the same church convention and disagree about how to vote on a given policy issue having to do with the use of pension funds, with the ordination of gays and lesbians, or with a social statement on ecology, land use, or capital punishment, how can these two have a constructive conversation? How can one take seriously the position of an opponent on anything with considerable moral density and argue one's own case energetically, but with respect for the other person's judgment? It certainly will not do to claim that one is more virtuous, or a person of superior character. It will not do to accuse, or even to imply, that the other lacks one's own degree of compassion or integrity. It might be possible to say that we don't do that in our family, our community, or our church. But even within a given tightly knit group with common memories and shared narratives, differences in moral judgment do occur. Is there anywhere to go other than to some authority within the group? How does such an authority emerge, and why should this authority's judgment be taken without question?

Adjudication among varying judgments is a problem, but it does not destroy character ethics as an extremely important option in ethical methodology. One thing is certain, that in order for there to be any interest in ethical reflection, there must first be an interest in morality. This interest presupposes some inner disposition to be a good person and to lead a good life. Character ethics advocates know that this cannot simply be assumed, that it has to be worked at within cohesive communities that care about it.

15. Making Methodological Commitments

Okay, now I know where you're coming from.

It is unhelpful to claim the use of all methodological options, or of no method at all. Helpful conversation advances when moral disputants are willing and able to state why and how they reach their conclusions to moral quandaries.

It has been stated that a case can be made for grouping methods for doing ethics into four major categories. The groupings described here are not arbitrary or the result of a purely personal desire to categorize things. Although, as has been stated, there are some disagreements among ethicists about these groupings and terms with which to designate them, the patterns of agreement are remarkable. The fact is that there are discrete options for doing ethics, whose special features can be described and grasped by anyone who cares to do so. These options have different ways of working through moral issues and cases and questions, and also of understanding what morality is fundamentally about. The hope is that the reader will at this point find the categories plausible and the descriptions understandable, and will have some confidence about seeing herself most closely described in one of these groupings.

For the sake of clarity, it is important to emphasize some qualifications that have already been briefly mentioned. One is that, although these are four discrete options that can be clearly differentiated from one another, it does not mean that they are totally monolithic structures having absolutely nothing to do with one another. They all have to do with morality, and they all have to do with taking moral matters seriously by being careful about how ethical reflection is done.

Some element of one may appear in a given practitioner's use of another. A given deontologist, for example, may demonstrate some interest in a probable outcome of a decision or an act, and may even make reference to this interest in a conversation. But in no case can a deontologist make a projected outcome the primary basis for what she considers to be a moral judgment, without abandoning deontology for teleology.

All deontologists pay attention to situations in order to apply universalizable rules. The application must be done carefully. Situations must be comparable in "morally relevant respects" in order for the application of the rule to be legitimate. Sometimes this process of application is called "casuistry."[1] But if the situation looms so large in the process that universal moral rules are exchanged for rules of thumb, and situations become the providers of data for the actual formulation of these rules, then deontology has been abandoned for situationism.

Similarly, as we shall see in Part 3, a teleologist most likely will be interested in formulating some exceptionless imperatives, that is, moral obligations that are taken to apply to a very broad spectrum of cases and situations. One particular way of doing this is sometimes called by philosophers "general rule utilitarianism." These imperatives differ from situationism's rules of thumb in that they carry far greater weight and are thought to be applicable to a great many cases and sustainable over long periods of time. They differ from the universal rules of deontology in that they are always tentative, subject to reformulation or even being overridden by the demands of new projected outcomes. The exceptionless imperatives of teleology also differ from the universal rules of deontology because they have been formulated not by reason alone, but with attention to data and projections that have affected the formulation of the rule. Not only deontologists work with rules. So also do situationists and teleologists. The point is that they formulate these rules on the basis of different criteria, and regard and use them in quite different ways.

Also, it is clear that everyone interested in morality and ethics has an interest in character and virtuous dispositions and attitudes, and that character ethicists have an interest in what people do as well as in who they are. Yet the distinction between character ethics and the other three options is clear when one sees where the focus is and how the process of ethical reflection plays out. The fact that some concerns are shared does not mean that the methods should be confused with one another.

It is important to say again how essential it is to remember that these methodologies are not vending machines. They do not deliver in any simple or direct way conclusions to moral quandaries. It is possible for people to arrive at opposite conclusions when using the same method, and to arrive at the same conclusion using different methods. It is a gross misuse of the discipline of ethics to hear a person's judgment in a particular case and to conclude without conversation that this means the person must be one or another kind of ethicist. The four methodological groupings are ways of working toward conclusions, not the conclusions themselves.

Some who encounter for the first time different strategies for ethical reflection on moral matters are inclined to think they all sound quite good. One may overlook the significant distinctions and simply jump from one to another arbitrarily as one or another item comes to mind. Others find the entire enterprise of ethical reflection to be so complicated and confusing that it is never taken seriously at all. One may even claim to have a superior hold on the correct conclusion to a moral issue or problem precisely because no method has been used to reach the conclusion, that it is somehow a simple and obvious moral truth.

The problem is that under such conditions conversations about important moral disagreements either do not occur, or else begin and go nowhere. There are probably few informed and interested people who have not found themselves in such a situation. A prediction of what will happen if a certain course of action is taken may be followed by a plea for understanding and compassion, which may be followed by a statement about the right thing to do, then a scolding that someone has not bothered to examine the facts of the matter. Along the way, assuming that the people trying to talk with one another are Christians, a Bible passage or two may be quoted. This may be countered by a passage that seems to express a different point of view. There may be appeals to folk wisdom, such as "Never say never," to which another may reply, "You just said it twice!" One may say, "He who hesitates is lost," and the other may reply, "Fools rush in where angels fear to tread." People who get involved in conversations such as this usually decide rather quickly that they have better things to do.

Methodological clarity among disputants in serious moral disagreement about matters of importance cannot guarantee civil and productive conversation, but it can help. If comments seem to come out of nowhere, if it seems impossible to move even for short periods of time from A to B, if no progress in understanding one another takes place, if all that happens is statement and counter-statement, it is all too discouraging. It is not worth anyone's time or effort. On the other hand, if people know who they are, where their fundamental commitments lie, how their moral stance and ethical method work, how to express all of this clearly, the conversation ought at least to be interesting. Someone may have an "ah ha!" moment and say, "Okay, now I know where you're coming from." It may bring about greater understanding and respect, and may possibly even move toward some kind of resolution.

The making of a methodological commitment is not an arbitrary process, but rather an exercise in self-discovery. As one contemplates genuine options, one may come to know better who one is, perhaps how one has changed over years, or possibly who one wants to be. These are not only different ways to do ethics, but different ways of reading the world. They represent not only different philosophical traditions, but also different understandings of what morality itself is about. When Christians are involved, these four ways of thinking about morality reflect different ways of reading the Bible, different ways of understanding what God is like and how God operates, different ways of assessing limits and possibilities of human agency. To think that one can switch from one method to another, even in the same conversation, would be equivalent to a Christian thinking she could be a Roman Catholic one day, a Pentecostal the next, and a Quaker the next. Such changes can and do take place over time, but not in a day, certainly not in a single conversation. Some degree of methodological clarity and consistency is essential if serious conversation is to take place about important moral disagreements.

The suggestion is that it is most helpful for a person interested in ethical reflection to find a method that seems to express the way one actually functions in moral matters. The next step is to explore as well as one can the presuppositions and working procedures of the method, and then to test it by thinking through some things in this way, and seeing whether it is possible to make one's position clear to another person. This can all be done tentatively. It does not mean that one has to stay with it for life. In fact, the spelling out of a particular method must include repeated references to the other methods, so that details can be specified and reasons can be clarified. It may even be that one will discover in the process that another method may turn out to be more congenial than the one first considered. For those with sufficient interest and energy, it is difficult to imagine a better exercise than to work through a recent volume, *Three Methods of Ethics: A Debate.*[2] The three methods debated are deontology, consequentialism, and character ethics. Should the reader wish to do as thorough a job also on situationism, there are several "debate" volumes referred to in the earlier chapter on this method.

We turn now to an exploration of consequentialism, a teleological method, including a discussion of how a consequentialist method might work for someone with Christian commitments. It is presented as an example of how a method may be developed rather than as a claim that this method is the best or most useful one. Some may find it an attractive option to consider as their own. Some not only may see many points along the way with which to take issue, but may find the proposal fundamentally unacceptable. The hope is that working through it with other possibilities in mind will be helpful to anyone seeking greater clarity in ethical reflection, regardless of the method to which one finds oneself most attracted.

Part Three

The Calculation of Consequences

16. Considering Consequentialism

Consider the consequences.

Consequentialism deserves consideration. It has problems, as do other methods of doing ethics. Yet it can be argued that differences about projected outcomes are what moral disputes are finally about.

———

It has been said repeatedly that this is a book about Christian Ethics. From the beginning it has been acknowledged that not only Christians lead moral lives and not only Christians think clearly and speak helpfully about moral matters. Thus Christians are obligated to work with those who are not Christians on issues that have to do with our common life and the health of this planet that we all share. In this section we shall consider consequentialism as an option for doing ethics, specifically acknowledging Christian commitments. As the subtitle of this book indicates, it is a way of understanding both morality and ethics in the context of the future. From a Christian perspective, the future is unthinkable apart from God's purpose in Jesus Christ for the entire created order. In regard to ethics, consequentialism is a teleological method.

Other options for doing ethics have been described in the previous section. An attempt was made to be both clear and fair. Each group of methodological options has worthy advocates and practitioners, including people with Christian commitments. This discussion of consequentialism is presented in some detail as an example of how one might work through more extensively some implications of one of the methodological groups. The hope is that it will be useful to those who reject consequentialism as well as to those who embrace it. In any case, thinking through how one does ethics in the context of other viable options should be a helpful exercise.

Consequentialism is sometimes used as a synonym for teleology. We have seen that the word "teleology" is derived from a Greek word, *telos,* which means "end" or "goal." As an ethical method, it says that one makes moral decisions and takes moral actions on the basis of a goal or end that one has in mind, toward which the action is designed to move. Consequentialism is an ethical method that says that the projected or anticipated consequences of an action are the most important thing to consider when making a moral judgment. We all say to one another from time to time, "Consider the consequences." Consequentialism says that, in moral matters, projected consequences are, finally, the most important thing to consider.

"Consequentialism" and "teleology" are sometimes used synonymously. They are sometimes distinguished. It may be said that teleology grounds moral decisions in long-term goals toward which the action is intended to move, and that consequentialism makes retrospective judgments about actions on the basis of actual consequences brought about. It seems to be a distinction without a difference, since any outcome-based ethical method must work with future projected outcomes, taking into account past experiences of how similar actions actually turned out.

We are using the word consequentialism here because it is more strictly an ethical category than is teleology, and because the intent is to construct a position for doing ethics in a Christian context, rather than to endorse what may by some be regarded as an outmoded way of doing science. Nevertheless, it is acknowledged that the two terms are closely associated with one another, and we shall be building upon the discussion of teleology presented in Part 2.

Teleology, when used in a broad way, often refers to an Aristotelian way of looking at reality. That is, it is often associated with an Aristotelian metaphysic. Aristotle thought that everything that exists, except God, is in motion from "potentiality" to "actuality." One can understand an acorn only if one knows that it is in motion toward becoming an oak tree, a baby only if one understands that it is in motion toward becoming an adult. Aristotle talked about God as "actus purus," that is, as purely actualized and thus with no potentiality and therefore with no motion. Another way Aristotle talked about God was as "prime mover unmoved." God is unmoved because God is in the perfect state of rest, but is prime mover because everything else, in motion, is being drawn by God into God's own place of absolute motionlessness, or complete rest.

This basic understanding of reality had implications not only for ethics, but for theology, biology, physics, astronomy, and every other arena of human enquiry. Aristotle's understanding of motion finally gave way to that of Newton and later to relativity theories that tied together space, time, and gravity. Motionlessness, or absolute rest, was no longer considered to be that place where potentialities are finally actualized. The Ptolemaic astronomy collapsed of its own weight once Galileo and others were able to make accurate observations of the movements of heavenly bodies. Our understandings of life forms have been revolutionized by Darwin and other evolution theorists, along with their supporters and critics. If teleological ethics is thought to be closely tied to Aristotelian metaphysics, and Aristotle's way of understanding reality is taken to be obviously obsolete, then teleology as a way of reflecting on the moral life is not going to be given much consideration.

"Consequentialism" thus serves our purpose better than does "teleology," because it is not so closely associated with a particular metaphysical or scientific paradigm and can be more easily focused on ethical concerns. It is true that consequentialism has everything to do with purpose and the future, and that consequentialism in a Christian context has everything to do with God's purpose for the entire created order, with the reality of evil, and also of the importance of human agency in the whole process. But this focus on purpose does not entail the adoption of Aristotelian teleology as a way of understanding reality.

There is a body of literature that deals with consequentialism as a method of doing ethics. One can find exquisite and detailed, although at times a bit esoteric, arguments for and against the position in a volume of essays titled *Consequentialism and Its Critics*, edited by Samuel Scheffler.[1] Since utilitarianism is a way of doing ethics that is closely allied to consequentialism, an investigation of utilitarianism can be helpful in the understanding and evaluation of this method. A useful discussion can be found in *Utilitarianism: For and Against*, a debate between J. J. C. Smart and Bernard Williams.[2]

In our attempt to consider consequentialism as a way of doing ethics in a Christian context, we are clearly moving away from deontology, situationism, and character ethics and embracing quite another way. We are saying that what is finally important in moral matters and in ethical reflection is the consequences, the results, the outcomes of decisions and actions. What we are proposing has connections with other "teleological" ethical methods, such as utilitarianism, pragmatism, and some variations of natural law theory. Thus the parameters of the consequentialism being considered should be quite clear—what is being rejected as unsatisfactory and what is being accepted as a broad framework within which to work.

There are difficulties, some more obvious than others. To begin, it seems at least precarious to take projections of future outcomes as the basis for something so essential to human identity as is morality. The future is unknown. When the oracle at Delphi in ancient Greece gave predictions to pilgrims seeking wisdom about the future, the oracle was very clever about saying things in such a way that the prediction could be claimed as true no matter what actually came to pass. It was something like opening a fortune cookie and reading, "Something good will happen for you." But moral judgments are not a trick or a joke. At some point we all take moral matters with great seriousness. An obvious problem is how something as important as morality can be based on something so elusive as projected outcomes. The future is so unpredictable, in fact, that this unpredictability has been formulated not only as "The Law of Unintended Consequences" but also as "Murphy's Law." The latter reads, "If anything can possibly go wrong, it will."

The consequentialist response is that absolute certainty is not available anywhere in this life, that living "under conditions of uncertainty" is what we all do, no matter what the activity. Yet we do not live in absolute uncertainty either. Whether we are doing physics or medicine, getting married or raising children, accepting a job offer or investing savings, making judgments about matters with high or low degrees of moral density, what we try to do is make informed judgments. There is information available, some past experience from which to learn, patterns to discern, expectations to clarify, probable outcomes to project.

Living without absolute certainty, but also without absolute uncertainty, applies even to Christian faith. In the Christian understanding of God and creation, faith is not "believing what we do not know," as though faith is absolutely certain because it is not based on human knowing. Christian faith is a perspective, a way of looking at everything including God and the creation, from the vantage point of the presence and power of God in Jesus Christ. It is taking everything with which we have anything to do and putting it together in the shape of the cross. It is, one could say, living a cruciform life. It is doing everything in the name of the Lord Jesus (Col. 3:17). Christians believe that the God who has been faithful in the past will continue to be faithful in the future. Working that through in moral matters is what ethical reflection in Christian context is about. Christian faith cannot be appropriately addressed with terms such as certainty and uncertainty. It is identical to neither and related to both. It has to do with the faithfulness of God and with our faithful response to that faithfulness.

Another obvious problem is that not every means can be justified to achieve a worthy end. There is a very guarded sense in which it is the end that justifies the means. Yet the Christian consequentialist can agree with deontologist Paul Ramsey when he says, "It can never *do any good* to do wrong or to intend to do wrong that good may come of it!"[3] But this is only the beginning of a conversation. In consequentialism, there are series of ends, all along the way from short to long term. There is a sense in which every end is in some sequence of various means, and every means is in some way an end result of previous acts and events. There is never just a single means and a single end.

In the context of the Christian mission, for example, it would be horribly contrary to Christian faith and life to torture and kill 10 percent of a village in order to force the remaining 90 percent to receive Christian baptism. The illustration seems ludicrous, except for the fact that such atrocities have on occasion been committed by Christians, perhaps with the thought that the end result would justify the action. One might hope that no Christian, quite apart from any notions of morality and ethics, would seek to justify such an action. The point here is that Christian consequentialism should reject such an action because every outcome imaginable is highly likely to be contrary to that which the Christian mission seeks to achieve. Lives would be snuffed out instead of given every possible opportunity to continue and flourish. Any remaining observer would see Christians doing exactly the opposite of what they say their founder told them to do. The event would be so remembered that those remaining who might receive baptism would in their hearts reject it. Any even quick projection of probable consequences of such an action should conclude that it would be disastrous precisely in terms of the result it would be intended to achieve. Christian consequentialists who know that God is active at all times and places in this world, that evil is also a pervasive reality, that human beings have been created as moral agents though whom God works to achieve God's purpose, also know that both means and ends are multiple and mutually dependent, and must be chosen in ways that each is seen to be compatible with the other.

Another obvious difficulty is that consequentialism as a way of dealing with moral matters sounds unacceptably heavy, far too demanding, excessively complicated, for something we expect everyone to respect and practice. How can busy people find time for this? How can a child or a person with limited capacities be expected to participate in such procedures or even follow such conversations?

A consequentialist may respond by first saying that there are consequentialist grounds for thinking that not every child and not every adult must do this kind of work. The consequences of a parent thinking that every word of counsel to a small child must be explained to the child's satisfaction may be far worse than the consequences of occasionally saying, "Because I said so." Growing up with some qualified sense of obedience to authority is not necessarily a bad thing. Yet responding to the question, "But why, Dad?" becomes increasingly important as the child grows, and teaching a child to take responsibility for the consequences of his or her actions is something almost every wise parent seeks to do. People with limited capacities also have limited responsibility for the consequences of their actions and even less responsibility for trying to figure out what those consequences may be. Busy people may well lead lives that affect the lives of many others, and thus have even greater than normal responsibility for weighing consequences of their actions, and also of taking time in their busy lives to work hard at figuring out what those consequences might be.

A consequentialist responding to the charge that the method is too complicated may go on to say that it is not necessary to reinvent the wheel every day. Moral wisdom is cumulative and often corporate. Patterns are developed, habits are formed, moral imperatives may be formulated, some far less tentative than others. We function in every other area of life by attempting to make choices on the basis of past experience, present observation, and future projections. The question may be asked why morality should be bracketed off into a place of its own, to be handled in a way different from everything else. Should not morality be at the center of life, affecting everything else and thus carried on in ways congruent with ways in which other things are understood and done?

The person who considers consequentialism to be the best way to do Christian Ethics knows that there are difficulties and objections to doing things this way. He believes, however, that there are satisfactory responses to these objections. Furthermore, he is convinced that differences in projected outcomes are finally what moral disputes are about.

The consideration of probable consequences seems to the consequentialist to appear with great frequency whenever there is serious disagreement about important matters, including matters with high degrees of moral density. It seems to be the case in matters of both foreign and domestic policy. If one thinks of debates about Northern Ireland, or how to move the peace process in the Middle East, whether the Gulf War was justified and whether it should have continued into Baghdad, what the appropriate response to Slobodan Milosevic and his actions should have been, or how to improve primary and secondary education or reform welfare or save Social Security, the consequentialist sees moral content in all of these and hears people at all levels arguing their opinions on the basis of projected probable outcomes of alternative scenarios. During the year-long "Monica Lewinsky affair," eloquent speeches were made and passionate columns written about what would probably come to pass if President Clinton were impeached, and by others on what would probably come to pass if he were not impeached. Who has not been in a discussion about the bombing of Hiroshima and Nagasaki in which the center stage was not occupied by statements from both sides having to do with consequences of this action, which everyone knows had massive moral content?

The consequentialist thinks this is also true in formal ethical disputes, that is, that deontologists, situationists, and character ethicists who are committed to their own methods do, finally, believe that their own methods yield the best results, the best moral conclusions, the most beneficial consequences. It sounds arrogant, and no consequentialist would expect advocates of other methods to agree, but neither would a consequentialist remain one if this were not his opinion.

A deontologist may formulate universal moral rules on the basis of reason alone, or may find these rules in what is thought to be a universal conscience, or in the Bible, or even written into nature. There is an explicit rejection of calculating consequences as a basis for moral decisions. Yet, when pressed, few deontologists are willing to leave it at the point of, "It's the right thing to do." As soon as the "why" question is pursued, it becomes apparent that projected outcomes are being factored into the equation. The reason that lying cannot be universalized by any rational person is because the entire social fabric would soon unravel, as would be the case if nobody kept promises.

There have no doubt been some pure situationists whose only value is tied to authentic existence based on the courage to dare one's own decisions and actions. Sartre may have been one such. But Joseph Fletcher is an example of a situationist who does not hesitate about arguing from projected consequences when he moves into the specifics of medical ethics, and even says specifically, "Only the end justifies the means; nothing else."[4] He is credited with almost inventing modern situationism yet moves quickly to consequences when arguing cases and issues.

Character ethicists are very clear that the focus of morality must be on the person rather than on the decision or the action. Yet they do not shy away from dealing with issues and cases, and when they do, they are not reluctant to state positions. How does it work? The argument is that if a person lives with a truly loving, or compassionate, or hopeful, or forgiving core of her being, it is inevitable that certain attitudes and actions will result. Hauerwas does not simply offer pacifism as one way that a person of Christian character may respond to conflict. He believes that it is the direction Christian character ought to move, and he argues his case, though often anecdotally, with probable outcomes clearly in mind.

Almost everyone says from time to time to oneself as well as to others, "Consider the consequences." Parents say it to children. Good friends say it to one another when seeking or giving counsel. People in high places with great power say it in the chambers of Congress and on CNN talk shows. People say it about serious matters, about decisions with very high degrees of moral density. Almost nobody thinks that considering consequences is simple. Yet few think it impossible. Consequentialists think that the consideration of consequences is so central to ethical reflection and moral action that consequentialism as an ethical method deserves to be considered. If something is "inconsequential," it is probably not worth the effort. If it is "a matter of consequence," it probably is worth the effort. Considering consequentialism in a Christian context is what this third section is about.

17. Consequentialism and Practical Wisdom

I'm sorry, but what you say doesn't make any sense to me.

Consequentialist ethics integrates empirical data, respects common sense, recognizes human imperfection, and embraces probability.

What is to be done in a conversation about an important disagreement with considerable moral density when one party says to another, "I'm sorry, but what you say doesn't make any sense to me"? Unfortunately, what often happens is that the conversation is terminated. It does seem to be a conversation stopper. On the other hand, the speaker does say, "I'm sorry," which should indicate a willingness to pursue the issue. If the person addressed decides to be gracious and to continue talking, how ought the conversation to proceed? Consequentialism suggests that the way to proceed is to try to state one's opinion in a way that attempts, at least, to make sense to the conversation partner. "Making sense" is very different from "reaching agreement." What the attempt to make sense may accomplish, as has been suggested, is to help the conversation partners "come to disagreement," a point without which serious conversation about important differences is impossible. Consequentialism is committed to practical wisdom. It is designed to make sense to common people who share common interests.

It is ironic that the criticism most often expressed against consequentialism has to do precisely with what consequentialism most energetically affirms, namely, that moral behavior and ethical reflection ought to be closely tied to practical wisdom. Although "practical wisdom" is sometimes used as a technical term in philosophical ethics, it is used here in a general sense to point to what people who value wisdom might think is a practical, rather than a theoretical, way to deal with moral matters. Situationism and character ethics can make valid claims about honoring "practical wisdom." It is with deontology that consequentialism at this point has its most serious disagreements.

If one traces these disagreements back to classical Greek philosophy, they can be understood as a decisive difference between Plato and Aristotle. Aristotle was a student of Plato, and worked with him in "The Academy" long before establishing his own school, "The Lyceum." It is possible to group them together under the theme of "Classic Greek Philosophy." There are similarities. It has been pointed out, for example, that the god of Aristotle is finally as motionless as is the god of Plato. But the differences are more decisive and more important for this discussion.

The artist Raphael captured those differences in his magnificent work "The School of Athens," which has its home in the Vatican Museum. Directly in the center of a large number of philosophers stand Plato and Aristotle. Plato points up, Aristotle points down. Plato agrees with the Pythagoreans and believes that the "real" is in the timeless realm above change and history. Aristotle agrees with Heraclitus that the "real" is in the observed realm that is known only when attention is paid to its motion through time and change. For Plato, truth, beauty, and goodness are defined in terms of changelessness. For Aristotle, these together with everything else, except God, are defined in terms of motion and development. The contrast has been noticed and commented on by many. Coleridge said that every person is born a Platonist or an Aristotelian. In *Consilience,* Edward Wilson draws the same division but calls it the difference between transcendentalism and empiricism.[1]

This fundamental difference can be traced throughout western history. It involves not only philosophy and ethics, but also Christian theology. It is a large oversimplification, but if the oversimplification is acknowledged, Augustine was a Platonist, and Thomas Aquinas an Aristotelian. Every point along the way is mixed, delicate, nuanced. Yet another oversimplification can be risked with some confidence. Deontology can be best understood on a line from Platonic Idealism through Kant and German Idealism to the present. Teleology can be best understood on a line from Aristotle to Thomas Aquinas to the Utilitarians to the present. Consequentialism and practical wisdom are clearly on that line that goes back to Aristotle rather than to Plato.

It has been argued here that the institution of morality cannot be entirely isolated from other social institutions, that it is more helpful to deal with a notion such as "degree of moral density" than to separate sharply the "moral" from the "non-moral," that finally all moral arguments depend on some claim about probable outcomes of attitudes and actions. The consequentialism to which these assertions point carries with it a number of corollaries.

One of these is that consequentialism integrates the use of empirical data into the process of doing ethics. For consequentialists, what is—and also what one thinks is going to be—is factored into what one thinks ought to be done now. Situationism pays great attention to what it considers to be the relevant data within a restricted time frame but specifically rejects attempts to project future outcomes. Character ethics cares a great deal about communities and shared narratives, and about the development of dispositions and virtues. Yet it rejects any focus on decision or action along with any attempt to project future outcomes.

It is with deontology that consequentialism is most obviously at odds regarding the use of empirical data in the doing of ethics. Not every deontologist is a pure Kantian, but every deontologist is sympathetic to Kant's essential commitments, and Kant was clear that every empirical drop must be squeezed out of the moral equation before a rule can be universalized.[2] He thought that what "is" the case must be clearly and cleanly separated from what "ought" to be done. This notion was later formulated by G. E. Moore in stark terms. He said that it is impossible to derive an "ought" from an "is." He labeled any attempt to do so "the naturalistic fallacy."[3] Nature, the observation of what is the case, empirical data, may be important for the application of moral rules, but in no case may they be factored into the formulation of the rules themselves.

There is an important body of literature concerning this "is/ought question" that has everything to do with the radical disagreement at this point between consequentialism and deontology.[4] When placed into the context of Christianity, it would be possible to look at Augustine as a representative of deontology. He considered the commands of God to be deontological rules. It is thus not surprising that he says, " . . .God's commands are to be submissively received, not to be argued against."[5] It is clear that any human opinion about what is or is probably going to happen, any observations or sense perceptions have nothing to do with moral behavior and ethical reflection. An

entirely different mood pervades the work of Aquinas. When discussing government, he says, "Look at the ants." When discussing
sexual matters, he says, "Look at the birds and the other animals."
Natural law models require the observation of nature in the process
of formulating moral rules. What ought to be done requires careful
observation of what is, in fact, the case. The created order, though
distorted by human sin, still bears the marks of its creator. Thus
something about God's will and intention can be discovered by careful observation of what God created and continues to create.

Consequentialism, although it includes a broad range of options
in ethical methodology, is at this point clearly on the side of Aquinas
rather than Augustine, of Aristotle rather than of Plato. Consequentialists believe that those things that are observable to human beings
about the nature of the case, about what is in fact going on, are of
great importance in figuring out what ought to be done. They affect
the process of anticipating probable outcomes.

Another ramification of linking consequentialism to practical
wisdom is the assertion that consequentialism respects common
sense. A definition of common sense may be uncommonly difficult to
come by. It may be like trying to define obscenity. Yet it is not
enough to say, "I know it when I see it" or "I know it when I hear it."
Such a response would be far too individualistic to fit with the position presented in this book.

One possible approach is to attempt to get at it negatively. That
is, there are people whose moral admonition is to do the right thing
whether it makes sense or not. In the political arena, a phrase is often
tacked onto a list of reasons for doing something. The phrase is, "and
because it's the right thing to do." In Christian circles this may be
expressed by saying, as did Augustine, that the will of God is to be
obeyed, not discussed. A biblical passage that comes to mind is the
word of Paul to the Corinthians, "God chose what is foolish in the
world to shame the wise" (1 Cor. 1:27). An obvious biblical story is
that of Abraham receiving the command of God to kill Isaac as a sacrifice. An extreme theological form of this idea can be found in Tertullian, who said, "*credo quia absurdum*," "I believe because it is
absurd." It would be quite inaccurate to equate consequentialism
with common sense, to suggest that every moral obligation must
make sense to everyone, that the word of God must be poured

through my own set of filters before I pay any attention to it. The point is rather that consequentialism respects common sense. It encourages common sense reflection upon moral obligations themselves, not just upon various applications of moral obligation that are thought to exist apart from common sense.

Perhaps it can be said this way. Consequentialism does ethics in a way that it believes will make sense to common people with common interests. Consequentialism abhors moral arrogance. It abhors moral elitism as much as it does a moral vacuum. It does not assume that its own way is automatically the right way, or that the conclusions of a particular consequentialist are the "right" conclusions. It does not assume that anyone who disagrees must be uninformed or inexperienced or unintelligent or insensitive or unaware or uncompassionate. It is not only willing, but it is eager to talk with those who disagree. Because it factors empirical data into the moral equation, it is interested in empirical data that come from the observations and opinions of those who disagree with its conclusions. It welcomes those assertions as additional information. Respecting common sense means respecting, not necessarily agreeing with, the moral judgments of common people who have common interests in morality as an indispensable social institution.

Another ramification of the congeniality of consequentialism and practical wisdom is that consequentialism recognizes the imperfection present in every human enterprise. On one level, this is a simple corollary of making use of empirical data and of respecting common sense. Almost anyone on the street will say from time to time that nobody is perfect. Imperfection is recognized to be intrinsic to the human condition. On another level, imperfection has to do with limits. Kant wrote about *Religion within the Limits of Reason Alone*.[6] Bernard Williams wrote about *Ethics and the Limits of Philosophy*.[7] Daniel Callahan has written about limits in the arena of health care for the aging and the dying.[8] Dietrich Bonhoeffer talked a great deal about limits of responsibility:

> We have now seen that the limit of responsible action lies in the fact that the deed ends in the grace and judgement of God and is bounded by the responsibility of our neighbours, and at the same time it becomes evident that it is precisely this limit which makes the action a responsible one. . . . It is precisely because it is not its

own master, because it is not unlimited and arrogant but crea-
turely and humble, that it can be sustained by an ultimate joy and
confidence and that it can know that it is secure in its origin, its
essence and its goal, in Christ.[9]

From the perspective of Christian faith, imperfection is named "sin,"
and this extends to rebellion against the will of God. We are using
the word "imperfection" here as a generic term to include a wide
range of meanings, including the Christian understanding of sin.

The point is that consequentialism works with what it considers
to be practical wisdom, and that practical wisdom assumes the presence of imperfection in every human enterprise. This is to say that
consequentialism is not an idealistic way of understanding morality
or of doing ethics. It does not deal with "moral ideals," nor does it
locate the "ought" out of sight in a realm totally separated from the
"is." It wants to side with "realism" rather than with "idealism."
Whether it uses the word *imperfections, limits,* or *sin,* consequentialism asserts that the human enterprise itself is an endeavor that
requires humility, not only about meeting moral obligations, but
about the making of judgments regarding what those moral obligations are. Both morality and ethics are human enterprises. Both are
always in motion, on the way, in the process of development. Neither
is simply given. Both need constant attention that implies the possibility of occasional revision.

One more ramification of the practical wisdom intrinsic to consequentialism is the embracing of probability rather than certainty. It
is important to acknowledge the fact that many Christians define
Christianity in terms of that which is certain in a vast sea of uncertainty. They sing with confidence, "Oh, Thou who changest not,
abide with me." Some people think that "matters of fact" are certain,
some people that "matters of morality" are certain. Consequentialists
believe that nothing is certain. Everything that exists, including
morality, exists in the context of probability.

Probability means living with degrees of uncertainty. As has
already been stated, some degree of uncertainty is intrinsic to any
way of life focused on the future. Of course, all knowledge is to some
degree perspectival, so we also live with some degree of uncertainty
regarding the past and even the present. But that does not mean living with total arbitrariness or chance. It does not mean abandoning

one's life to fate. Consequentialism, committed to practical wisdom, empirical data, common sense, and the recognition of imperfection inherent in the human enterprise, is also committed to living in the real world, embracing probability in moral as well as all other arenas of human existence.

Werner Heisenberg's "Principle of Uncertainty" can serve as a paradigm. Heisenberg insisted that it is impossible to determine the position and momentum of a subatomic particle in a system. The measurement of one affects the measurement of the other. But it is possible to make statements about the total system that are very, but not absolutely, accurate. Probability is a positive way of talking about uncertainty. At the same time that we say we do not know anything with absolute certainty, we can say that we do know a great many things with very high degrees of probability. The discipline of statistics has to do with probabilities. "Standard deviations" and "bell curves" have to do with probabilities. Actuarial experts cannot say anything about the death of an individual and cannot be absolutely certain even about precise numbers for averages in large populations. Longevity expectations are rising, but nobody knows with absolute certainty what that rate is or will be in twenty years. Yet insurance premiums and payouts work fairly well on the basis of probabilities.

Consequentialists embrace probability in the moral life as they believe almost everyone else does in every other arena of human existence. Morality is not so strange a phenomenon, they think, that it has to be projected into some realm other than that of the commonly human. For Christians, morality has to do with its common confession of the universe as God's handiwork, the enfleshment of God in Jesus of Nazareth, the resurrection of the body. Christians also know a great deal about sin. It helps to keep them from attempting to live in any other than in this real, actual, imperfect world. Christians know about the living God, the risen Jesus, and the moving Spirit. It helps them to live always with hope, even in this messy and ambiguous time and place. Christians have every reason to embrace practical wisdom, perhaps even consequentialism.

18. A Unified Field Theory of Ethics

Only connect.
> —*E. M. Forster,* Howard's End

Among available options, consequentialism provides the greatest promise for constructing a unified field theory of ethics, one that can deal gracefully with the full range of micro to macro moral issues.

━━━　～━

This is a book about Christian Ethics. Consequentialism is being explored as a way of doing ethics in a Christian context. In this chapter, it will be stated that there is a remarkable congruity between the cosmic sweep of the Christian claim and the adaptability of consequentialism to deal with moral issues everywhere and at any point within that entire range.

The Christian Bible and all of the ecumenical creeds—the Apostles', the Nicene, the Athanasian—begin with an affirmation that everything that exists was brought into being by one God. That totality is not limited to planet Earth and certainly not to human beings. The statements are clear that whatever there is exists only because God made it and continues to make and sustain it. The statements are declarative and doxological. All of the how and when questions are left open to be explored and debated.

The statements are also clear that everything that was made good has been disturbed, distorted, put out of joint (Gen. 3:1-24). It is human beings, created in God's image (Gen. 1:26f) to reflect God's care for God's good creation and to "care for the garden" (Gen. 2:15), who misused the gift of their freedom and who bear responsibility for the current distorted state in which they and everything else now exist. That misuse of freedom continues to distort and even to destroy not only human life, but the life of God's creation.

The Christian Bible and the entire Christian tradition are also clear that God did not in anger abandon the work of his creative power, but in continuing love has moved and continues to move decisively in its favor. The story of God's promise and its fulfillment in Jesus incarnate, crucified, and risen, along with the granting of God's Holy Spirit, is the story of God's total involvement with the total creation continuing from the beginning through the present and on into the future.

The Christian claim is that there is one God who is the creator and the redeemer of one creation. The human story is played out in the center of this cosmic drama. The fact that God is triune tells us that there is no unity without diversity. It is a specifically Christian doctrine. The God proclaimed by the Christian confession would not be one God were this one God not three persons—Father, Son, and Holy Spirit. So also the one creation would not be one creation if it were not marked by diversity, in this case infinite diversity. The same unity and diversity marks the church, which is one body with many members. If the body were only one member, it would not be a body (1 Cor. 12:12-31). Thus the Christian is one member of the many-membered Body of Christ who worships the one triune God and seeks to get in on the continuing work of this creating and redeeming God wherever possible in the midst of this one awesome and infinitely diverse creation.

So how shall Christians think about morality, do what they can to be moral people, behave in ways that they and others will consider to be moral behavior? How shall Christians do ethics that is for them and for others in some way, at least, recognizably Christian? It has to be possible to be unapologetically Christian in one's faith and life and, not in spite of, but because of that fact, to be at the same time in serious conversation about important moral matters with people who do not share Christian commitments. The suggestion here is that consequentialism provides the greatest promise to accomplish this because it deals with the same real world with which every human being deals and has a perspective on the world that desires to learn from the past and to press forward into the future.

We began with the doctrine of creation to be clear that Christianity is not pantheism. God is not everything, and everything is not God. Christianity is not either religious or philosophical dualism. It is not the case that good and evil are equally powerful forces forever at odds with one another, and it is not the case that reality is split in two, into the empirical or material on the one hand and the transcendent or spiritual on the other. Since Christianity proclaims that the Word became flesh (John 1:14), there can be no absolute split between value and fact, between "ought" and "is." Nor is Christianity the monism that treats everything other than the One as an emanation that becomes lesser and lesser, dimmer and dimmer, as it moves farther and farther away, as does light from its source. The Christian doctrine of creation is a specifically Christian perspective on everything and on the God who has to do with everything. If it is the case, as has been argued here, that there is nothing with absolutely no moral content, that every issue is, potentially at least, an issue with considerable moral density, then Christian faith and life ought to have something to offer to a way of considering the full range of moral issues in a graceful way. We are talking about the move toward the construction of such a position as a move toward what might be called a unified field theory of ethics.

The term, of course, comes from physics. Albert Einstein was able to put the theory of relativity into a single elegant formula, $E = mc^2$, energy equals mass times the square of the constant, which is 186,000 miles per second, the speed of light. It was a tribute to the genius of Einstein. It was also an act of praise to the unity of this vastly diverse creation. Einstein was not a Christian, but he did not hesitate to make references to God. He expressed his confidence in the unity of creation again in a simple formula when he said, "God does not play dice with the universe."

Einstein worked primarily with very large astronomical systems in which gravitational forces were an essential factor, systems in which Newtonian understandings of space and time failed to function with any degree of accuracy. Werner Heisenberg worked with subatomic particles, where Newton also was not helpful. We have already mentioned Heisenberg's principle of uncertainty. Yet it was and is possible to work with larger systems of particles and to make highly accurate determinations of how they function. The physicists who worked to split the uranium atom, to start chain reactions, and eventually to create the atom bomb, did not do so working with total or absolute uncertainty about what they were doing.

Nevertheless, no physicist or mathematician has thus far managed to place into a single formula the workings of the entire physical order, from the outer edges of space beyond the reaches of any telescope to the inner space in which the tiniest particles, beyond the reach of any microscope, swirl in random and unpredictable ways. There are those who continue to work on it. Some theoretical physicists pursue the goal of the final theory, the theory of everything, or T.O.E., as it is often called. Stephen W. Hawking has devoted his genius to the project of bringing together black hole theory and quantum mechanics. His esoteric work became a matter of great public interest with his publication of *A Brief History of Time*. He concludes, "However, if we do discover a complete theory . . . if we find the answer to that, it would be the ultimate triumph of human reason—for then we would know the mind of God."[1]

There are philosophical pluralists, who believe that reality is intrinsically, inexorably, relentlessly pluralistic—incapable of ever being grasped in one way because it is itself composed of irreconcilable, opposing, incommensurate components. Physicists who believe this also believe that Einstein's and Hawking's work toward a unified field theory of the physical order is futile because it is, in the nature of the case, impossible. It is a fascinating and complicated debate. Isaiah Berlin has divided people into two categories, hedgehogs and foxes, saying the fox knows many things, but the hedgehog knows one big thing. Berlin says he is a fox, a pluralist. An interesting twist is that some argue that pluralism is itself a unifying way of understanding reality.[2]

Nevertheless, whatever the debates in physics and philosophy, it is striking that in the same half century the United States embarked on a program to put an astronaut on the moon and to map the human genome, to determine the place of every gene on the human DNA. The first was successfully accomplished in 1969. It is now probably only a matter of a few years until the second project will be accomplished. There may be some sense in which we live in a "pluralistic universe," but the fact is that scientists, regardless of the field of investigation or the project proposed, work with essentially the same patterns of observing and collecting data, formulating hypotheses, testing these experimentally and theoretically, and allowing intuitions to play with materials toward formulations that serve to predict outcomes with some degree of accuracy. The philosophical questions about the unity or the pluralism of reality need not be finally solved in order either to put an astronaut on the moon or to map the human genome.

The question is whether it is possible to bring any coherence to the discipline of ethics, which is, at best, almost unbelievably diffused. It is a limited goal. There is no expectation here that any amount of ethical reflection will produce a procedure by which everyone concerned with a given moral issue or case will come to agree with one another on what ought to be done. Even if possible, there is good reason to doubt that such a state of affairs would be very interesting or productive. The question has to do rather with whether some degree of common and coherent understanding of what ethics is about, perhaps analogous to that relatively common and coherent understanding of what science is about, can be achieved. The question includes, in this context, whether Christian commitments about faith and life may have anything to contribute to such an understanding.

Ethics is not physics. But it is a human enterprise of great importance to vast numbers of people. Unfortunately, it is diffused in almost every direction and at every level. We have discussed in Part 1 the problems of language usage, including the difficulty of even arriving at an understanding of morality itself. We saw that the word "ethics" is often used, in many contexts, not to designate the discipline that seeks to understand and work in helpful ways with morality, but as a synonym for morality.

Thus, medical ethics, whether in a book or an article, a lecture or a session of a medical ethics committee, often is marked by clusters of opinions and judgments about moral matters related to the practice of medicine, without any attention to presuppositions and procedures, to method, to those "why" and "how" questions that lie behind the conclusions. It can be immensely interesting and enlightening. Often there is exquisitely detailed analysis of issues and options, perhaps of a particular case. People who function at this level have usually learned to be civil and respectful toward one another. But is it ethics that is being done if there is nothing said about how one goes about what one is doing and why one does it as one does? This is by no means to suggest that methodological questions are never addressed, only to say that they are not addressed very often. When decisions have to be made in the context of significant disagreement, the absence of methodological clarity on the part of those who disagree leaves open only resort to a vote or to acquiescence to the opinion of the person considered to be the best authority.

The extraordinarily diffused nature of the ethics enterprise is evident in every direction and at every level. What is the case in medical ethics is also true in business ethics, probably even more so. Legal ethics is still a term that refers more often to codes of conduct designed to retain public trust than to any gathered attempt to think through in helpful ways the intricate interrelationships of law and morality, and how each ought to do its work with regard to the other. Environmental ethics defines an area of concern. It is not always clear how the work done or the conversations held differ in any significant way from activities by environmentalists who work with no particular claim to be doing ethics.

One thinks of other designations, such as liberation ethics, postmodern ethics, feminist ethics, philosophical ethics, religious ethics, or even Christian Ethics. In all of these and the above cases, "ethics" is the noun that is somehow qualified by an adjective. The question we are asking is whether it is possible to bring any coherence to this very diffused discipline, any way of speaking about ethics itself that could serve as a candidate, at least, for a generic understanding of the task.

The suggestion here is that consequentialism is a way of doing ethics that could serve as such a candidate. Whether the question is how to allocate kidneys to those waiting for transplants or whether to do prenatal gene replacement therapy, whether to send manned or unmanned missions into space, how much of the federal budget should be spent finding out what we can about Mars, it is difficult to imagine anyone seriously objecting to factoring into the discussion probable costs and probable benefits. Differences in projections can be talked about on the basis of available data and past experiences. Varying estimates about costs and benefits can be discussed in the context of expressed goals, which can be clarified and defended when the request is made to do so. The process can be carried out in an atmosphere of mutual respect, since it is a common-sense method of problem solving, and everyone should be able to agree that a common desire is to bring about as good a result as possible. There is no need to shift gears, to change one method for another, to jump from one presupposition to the next. It is possible to see consequentialism functioning across the full range of micro to macro moral issues and making sense no matter what the adjective is that in the conversation modifies the noun "ethics."

The suggestion is that Christians may have specific and ample materials with which to work to warrant the consideration of consequentialism as a method that can serve as some kind of unified field theory of ethics. The Christian doctrines of the triune God, the total created order, and the Christian as responsible moral agent all contribute to the suggestion. There is one God, one creation, one church. But each can be understood only as unity within diversity. Ethics is not physics, and a unified field theory of ethics does not depend on the achievement of a unified field theory of the physical order. But bringing some coherence to the very diffused discipline of ethics should be of interest to many. The famous line "Only connect" in *Howard's End* refers to people. Most of us think, however, that everything is somehow connected to everything else. The task is to work at those connections in our understanding of morality and in the doing of ethics.

19. Calculating Probable Outcomes

You'd better learn calculus. It's the language that God speaks.
—*Herman Wouk,* Inside Outside

Biblical support for deontology, situationism, and character ethics is not difficult to find. It is quite possible, however, to ground consequentialism in the whole message of the whole Bible, as well as in specific passages.

———

All Christians regard the Bible as an important resource for Christian life as well as for Christian faith, although they think about and make use of the Bible in very different ways.[1] The history of biblical interpretation and the variety of hermeneutical options currently available are fascinating. Biblical support for ethical methodologies other than consequentialism may seem rather obvious.

Deontologists can find ample examples of unqualified imperatives that can be read as universal moral rules. One can begin with the Ten Commandments. But there are a great many others. Very broad exhortations include "Do justice, love kindness, and walk humbly with your God" (Mic. 6:8), and "You shall love the Lord your God with all your heart and soul and mind, and your neighbor as yourself" (Matt. 22:27-40). Many seem to be very specific, such as "Let every person be subject to the governing authorities; for there is no authority except from God, and those authorities that exist have been instituted by God" (Rom. 13:1), or "If someone wants to . . . take your coat, give your cloak as well" (Matt. 5:40). It is possible to take such unqualified imperatives as words from God, or as the Word of God in some more complicated sense, or even as counsel formulated by faithful people touched by God's Spirit. It is possible then to handle these imperatives in various ways. Whatever the particulars are, it is clear that deontology can find biblical support if it wishes to do so.

Likewise, Christian situationists can find numerous stories in the Bible that illustrate the situational nature of appropriate actions. A situationist could move from the extreme example of Abraham and

the sacrifice of his son Isaac (Gen. 22:1-19) to the captivating story
told by Jesus about the Good Samaritan (Luke 10:29-37). It is possible to read the Bible as a long series of stories that illustrate both
appropriate and inappropriate responses to the demands of given situations. One can also construct an impressive theological framework
for situationism, as did Rudolf Bultmann, making use of an existentialist method of biblical interpretation.

Christian character ethicists make abundant and careful use of
biblical resources. There are community narratives and shared memories. There are extensive stories of families and stories of extended
families. There are depictions of exemplary character development
and of development that goes badly. Many sayings of Jesus fit in
very nicely, and there are actual lists of virtues in the writings of the
apostle Paul. Deontologists, situationists, and character ethicists
have no problem finding biblical support for their methodological
commitments.

Consequentialism as a way to describe the Christian life, as a biblical way to understand morality and to do ethics, may seem not to
be so obvious. Not every Christian makes an immediate connection
between calculating probable outcomes and taking up one's cross
and following Jesus. The very word "calculating" seems to some to
describe the kind of person a Christian is not. In common usage,
"calculating" tends to refer to a person who is not straightforward,
who may hold back emotions while thinking too much about how
others may react, who may even be figuring out how to turn things
to his own advantage while giving the impression that a light and
easy conversation is taking place. It is usually not a compliment to
say of someone, "He's a very calculating person."

On the other hand, we have seen many cases in which words mean
very different things in different contexts. A Christian may say with
enthusiasm and gratitude, "Our pastor can really preach!" The same
person may on some other occasion scold a friend by saying, "Don't
preach at me." Slight changes can make large differences in meaning.
"She's a very moral person" is a compliment. "She's a very moralistic
person" is a complaint. Saying of someone that he is a calculating
person usually sends negative signals about that person. But this
does not mean that making calculations is always a bad thing.

In fact, we make formal and informal calculations about a great
many things in daily life, and some of these are very important.

Almost all of them have some reference to past experience, and many have specific futures in mind. Not many families try to get along without a pocket calculator. It is often there along with pens and paper clips as standard equipment on the desk, or near the kitchen table, or wherever the household finances are managed. We file income tax returns, pay bills, make decisions about insurance policies and mortgages, and plan for possible emergencies, college costs, and retirement needs. It is difficult to imagine anyone thinking that carefully calculating such things is a bad idea.

We make calculations informally whenever we anticipate possible problems and attempt to act so as to avoid them. Good drivers do not tailgate other vehicles, but constantly calculate and recalculate, automatically, a reasonable following distance factoring in speed, weather, road conditions, traffic. People who value kindness do not necessarily avoid offending others at all costs, but do pay attention to emotional reactions of conversation partners, and move to less forceful speech when tempers begin to flare. Those who care about others who are affected by their decisions and actions do not just fall in love and get married. They do the best they can first to figure out how such a marriage is likely to work in the long run, realizing that even then things may turn out badly. Only very foolish people or those with very limited capacities refuse to make any calculations when dealing with important matters.

But what about calculations and morality? It is being proposed here that morality is not a strange phenomenon to be bracketed off into its own special space apart from the "non-moral." Morality is taken to be a social institution that has a great deal to do with other social institutions and every facet of life. There are degrees of moral density, but nothing with absolutely no moral content whatsoever. The fact that this places morality and ethics in close proximity to practical wisdom is taken to be a plus, not a minus. Prudence, the attempt to act wisely with the future in mind, is taken to be a virtue having everything to do with living a moral life and reflecting on it carefully. Calculating probable outcomes is quite simply a normal part of this whole process.

Christian consequentialists use the Bible as an important resource for faith and life, as do other Christians. There is no immediate or direct line from the Bible to any method of understanding morality and doing ethics. Yet it would be difficult to claim that what one is doing is Christian unless it is possible to point to some connections between it and the Bible. Furthermore, it is clear that such connections cannot be forced or artificially construed. Christians ought not first to decide what to believe and how to live and then see whether they can find some support for their decisions somewhere in the Bible. There needs to be a recognition of the Bible as a primary resource and an honest attempt to discover what these documents have to say. There is every reason to assume that Christian practitioners of deontology, situationism, and character ethics do exactly this, and are convinced that their way of doing things is grounded in serious biblical investigation.

Various Christians doing ethics in a variety of consequentialist ways may make different kinds of appeal to the Bible. The claim here is that it is possible to say something valid about the whole message of the whole Bible. There are those now working in biblical studies who consider the very thought of talking about this big picture approach to be problematic, if not simple minded or even wrong headed. Some regard the diversities in the biblical documents to be so overwhelming that some things must be rejected as other things are embraced. Some say that the text does not even exist except in the interpretation of the reader, something like "beauty is in the eye of the beholder." Some think it necessary to "deconstruct" a text, using the "hermeneutics of suspicion" to make clear that those who wrote the documents did so wanting to retain their positions of power. Nevertheless, even in the current jungle of biblical interpretation, it is not necessary to be apologetic about reading the whole Bible looking for that whole message upon which to base the Christian faith and life.

Throughout the Bible there are stories of individuals and groups living with consequences, both good and bad, of their actions. There are expressions of God's will with promises attached, and these promises are often conditional. How things turn out is not a result of arbitrary actions of God toward people who do or do not do what God says to do. How things turn out has something to do with consequences that come, not inevitably or always or automatically, but often nevertheless, in part because people have chosen to behave as they do. The creation has been ordered by the Creator, and there remains some essential congruity between Creator and creation even though this congruity is distorted by sin. To oppose the Creator is to oppose the creation, and this cannot be done with impunity. "What goes around comes around" is not a Bible verse. Even as a piece of folk wisdom, it has to be qualified considerably before being embraced. Yet consequentialists are apt to think that the truth it expresses is present in biblical stories that take human agency very seriously.

The big picture into which these stories fit tells us that the God who brought all things into existence, and has remained faithful to the people of God even when they have been unfaithful, will continue to care for and remain faithful to the entire creation until that time when the purpose of God is complete. It is a story that has to do with everything and that stretches from beginning to end, from alpha to omega. The purpose of God is described in many ways, but it has to do with the fixing of that which needs fixing, the reconciling of that which is alienated, the healing of that which is ill, the releasing of that which is in bondage, the making whole of that which has disintegrated. The God of the Bible is known not by separation from time, not by occasional episodic interventions into time, not by involvement only in the internal lives of individuals, but rather by total involvement in the total creation, at work in every time and every place. Christians remind themselves of this big picture every time they join in confessing their faith in the words of one of the great creeds of the church. Living the Christian life in this context means to be aware of the work God is doing in God's creation and to seek to get in on it as effectively as possible.

This is not to suggest that the documents in the Bible are arranged in a strictly chronological way, that every piece of the story is equally important, or that every story should be read as an accurate portrayal of a piece of chronological history. It is rather to say that the whole Bible tells a whole story and that this story is about God and God's work with and purpose for the whole creation. It is hardly a novel idea. Christians have read the Bible in essentially this way for centuries. It is evident in the ecumenical creeds and in confessional statements and other documents that various Christian traditions regard as reliable summaries of the content of the biblical documents.

Various parts, then, take their meaning in the context of the whole. One does not forget the big picture when going to work on the details. A fruitful place to go in order to see how this works in a particular setting is the apostle Paul's first letter to the congregation at Corinth. After the Thessalonian correspondence, it is probably the earliest document in the New Testament, written about A.D. 55, prior to the time that any of the four Gospels was written. It gives us an intimate glimpse of how the earliest church, only twenty years after the death and resurrection of Jesus, actually functioned. In addition, it may be the document in the New Testament most specifically dedicated to ethical reflection. We can take a brief look.

Paul spent eighteen months in Corinth preaching and gathering together a congregation of believers (Acts 18:1-11). After he left, problems arose and the people needed Paul's help. First Corinthians is Paul's response to these problems, primarily problems about behavior. There are two sets, one set delivered to Paul personally by "Chloe's people" (1 Cor. 1:11), the other brought to him in a "written report" (7:1). Paul clicks off his responses to the problems one by one. The first three (quarreling, sexual misbehavior, legal disputes) are signaled by an introductory "It is reported." The next set (marriage and single life, eating meat that has been on pagan altars, speaking in tongues, the resurrection of the dead, offerings for the churches in Jerusalem) is signaled by an introductory "Now concerning. . . ."

In each case, the people want Paul to tell them who in the dispute is right and who is wrong. In each case, with the exception of the sexual misbehavior in chapter 5 and notably the resurrection issue in chapter 15, Paul responds with an "it all depends." That on which it all depends is the anticipated outcome. Paul refuses to say who is right and who is wrong. He goes back and forth, "on the one hand" and then "on the other hand." His response to their problems is, essentially, "Consider the consequences, and make your decision on the basis of your best projection of anticipated outcomes."

Paul's response to quarreling (1:11–4:21) is that it does not matter through whom these people heard the gospel. What matters is the cross of Jesus, which binds them together. Even God does things with a purpose in mind. "God chose what is foolish in the world to shame the wise . . . so that no one might boast in the presence of God" (1:27-29), that is, so that people will place their confidence in Christ and not in their own wisdom. It is clear that it is fine to be married or single (7:1-40). What is wrong is to think that either state is required. The reason that it is possible to sit loose on this issue, to "live as though not" (7:29-31), is the future perspective that feeds back into the present.

Concerning the eating of meat that may have been on a pagan altar (8:1–11:34), it is clear that they may or may not eat it. They should think about with whom they are eating, about whether what they do may damage another's faith, about their motives for doing what they do. It depends on how they calculate the probable consequences of their actions. In this context Paul explains that his own very great flexibility is based not simply on differing situations, but specifically with a purpose in mind: "I have become all things to all people, that I might by all means save some. I do it all for the sake of the gospel" (9:22-23). Should they speak in tongues (12:1–14:40)? They may or they may not. Paul says it all depends on whether this activity will build up or tear down the church (14:5, 12, 26). Even this religious practice is treated in terms of probable outcomes. When it comes to a matter of faith and confession, the resurrection of the dead on the last day (15:1-58), there is no room to maneuver. If the end, the *eschaton,* the *telos,* is rejected, everything is lost (15:12-19). Paul's comments in this letter are straightforward and practical. It is an important resource for any Christian interested in morality and ethics.

Some of the sayings of Jesus sound simple and absolute. He says that if anyone asks you for something, give it to him (Matt. 5:40). One way to treat this is to think it is the "ideal" way to behave if one is truly a loving person, and then to feel guilty that one does not actually do it. It is not the only way to read this text. The *Didache,* a very early Christian document, comments on this text in this way: "Let your alms sweat in your hands until you find out to whom to give."[2] In other words, think about it first, whether or not it will actually help the person. Luther's comment on these words of Jesus are similar. He says that Jesus means, "Give to the one who really needs it." He continues to say there are too many people who want to take everything a person has and leave that person without the means to take care of his own family. Luther says that Jesus obviously intends that if the person asking is a scoundrel, he should not be given what he asks for.[3] The *Didache,* Luther, and a great many others have understood Jesus to assume that consequences would be considered and calculated. Most Christians agree. Christian stewardship, for example, is not just a matter of gratitude to God, or the need to be a giving person. Most Christians give with serious reflection about what is likely to be accomplished with their gift.

There is good reason to read some of the short and seemingly simple aphorisms of Jesus in this way. Jesus tells his followers to "count the cost" (Luke 14:28-33), to be "wise as serpents" at the same time that they are "innocent as doves" (Matt. 10:16). There are numerous references to probable outcomes. His followers should build their houses on rock rather than on sand, in order to anticipate rough weather (Matt. 7:24-27). They should let their lights shine for a purpose, that people will observe their actions and glorify God (Matt. 5:16). Even when taking a seat at a banquet table, they should do it keeping in mind what may happen when other guests arrive (Luke14:7-11). Was Jesus a consequentialist? Of course, the Christian who reads the Bible this way does not shrink from replying that he was.

The living God of the Bible (Heb. 3:12; 9:14; 10:31; 12:22) acts purposefully, with a goal in mind, an end in view. This God plans, speaks, acts. The human beings to whom God has given considerable freedom frequently frustrate God's work. The living God does not hesitate changing course, making mid-course corrections, changing his mind (Jer. 18:8, 10; 26:3, 13) and moving on. It happens repeatedly. It may not be an entirely outrageous anthropomorphism to suggest that the God of the Bible calculates consequences then recalculates to adjust to changing circumstances.

One character starts to teach another about calculus in Herman Wouk's novel *Inside Outside,* saying, "That's the language God speaks, you'd better learn it."[4] The mathematical science of the calculus goes far beyond the mechanical work done by a pocket calculator. By differentiating and integrating infinitely small slices of whatever it is that is being examined, it describes reality in motion. It calculates rates of change in the system being studied. The exponential rise in technological achievements that we witnessed in the twentieth century could not have happened without the help of this tool developed in the seventeenth century by Isaac Newton and G. W. Leibniz. The Creator and the creation have a great deal to do with one another. Calculus is an exquisite tool for describing the reality in motion that is the creation. It may make some sense to say that calculus is the language that the Creator speaks.

Christians have a great stake in this real world that is God's creation. With the perspective they have on Creator and creation, it is not strange that they should reflect on which behaviors to encourage and which to discourage by attempting to calculate probable outcomes, making educated guesses, and proceeding with caution. Sharon D. Welch has written *A Feminist Ethic of Risk.*[5] There are always risks. The consequentialist position being developed here could be called "a Christian ethic of calculated risk." We live with probabilities rather than certainties. This is all the more reason that we should attempt to be wise, to act prudently, to avoid stupid mistakes and, if possible, irreversible errors. All of this has everything to do with Jesus Christ, in, through, and for whom all things were made and through whom all things are being reconciled to God (Col. 1:15-20).

20. Jesus Christ and the Future of God's Creation

All things have been created through him and for him. . . . And whatever you do, in word or deed, do everything in the name of the Lord Jesus.
—Colossians 1:16b; 3:17

The cosmic purpose of God in Jesus Christ is theological ground for the construction of a consequentialist ethic that seeks to do all things in congruity with that purpose.

———

Christians have for centuries read the whole Bible seeking to come to grips with its total message. It has seemed clear that this message has to do with the total history of the entire creation, from beginning to end. One way in which this has been expressed is in terms of promise and fulfillment. It has seemed abundantly clear that at the center of this entire cosmic drama is the person and work of Jesus Christ.

The church was quick to realize that it could not deal adequately with Jesus of Nazareth by treating him as a great teacher of morality. It soon formulated a confession that served well both to identify who they believed Jesus to be, and also to identify those who did so believe. The confession was "Jesus is Lord." No Jewish person said this lightly, because "Lord" *(Adonai)* was a term used to refer to Jehovah God. No Roman said this lightly, because "Lord" was a term used to refer to the emperor, Caesar. Thus "Jesus is Lord" became the earliest Christian confession. Paul writes in his letter to the congregation in Rome, "If you confess with your lips that Jesus is Lord and believe in your heart that God raised him from the dead, you will be saved" (Rom. 10:9). When responding to the congregation at Corinth to their question about speaking in tongues, he tells them that the true test of the presence of the Holy Spirit in a person's life is the clear confession that Jesus is Lord (1 Cor. 12:1-3).

As the church dealt with all of this, a doctrine of God as triune began to emerge, and soon there were trinitarian formulas circulating in the early congregations. One can find it in the baptismal formula in the "great commission" in Matthew's Gospel. "Go . . . make disciples . . . baptizing in the name of the Father and of the Son and of the Holy Spirit . . . and teaching . . ." (Matt. 28:19-20). It is also there in early benedictions. "The grace of the Lord Jesus Christ, the love of God, and the communion of the Holy Spirit be with all of you" (2 Cor. 13:13). The awareness of God as triune grew gradually, but a detailed doctrine of the triune God was not crafted until a few centuries later when clarification became necessary in the context of multiple misunderstandings. The key document that emerged is what we known as the Nicene Creed. It is further detailed in the Athanasian Creed.

The history and development in the midst of controversies is, of course, complex.[1] Yet the confession is clear. There is one God, and this one God is three persons. A later clarifying formula that developed was: "The internal works of the triune God are divisible; the external works are indivisible" (*Opera ad intra sunt divisa; opera ad extra sunt indivisa*). It means that, for the sake of affirming the threeness, it is important to make internal distinctions, such as "the Son is begotten of the Father," "The Spirit proceeds from the Father and the Son."[2] For the sake of affirming the oneness, it is important to be clear that it is the one triune God who creates, redeems, and sanctifies.

Thus, because Jesus Christ is the center of the whole message of the whole Bible, and because the triune God is one God, it is not strange that Jesus Christ is seen by the New Testament church to be the agent of the creation and redemption of all things. It is clear in the prologue to the fourth Gospel:

> In the beginning was the Word, and the Word was with God, and the Word was God. . . . All things came into being through him, and without him not one thing came into being. . . . And the Word became flesh and lived among us. . . . (John 1:1-3, 14)

It is clear in the prologue to the letter to the Hebrews.

> Long ago God spoke to our ancestors in many and various ways by the prophets, but in these last days he has spoken to us by a Son . . . through whom he also created the worlds. (Heb. 1:1-2)

It is also clear in the letter to the Ephesians.

The place where the proclamation of Jesus Christ and the future of God's creation is most magnificently expressed is in the letter to the congregation at Colossae. Anyone interested in understanding the Christian faith and life in terms of God's total purpose and our response to that purpose will benefit from a careful examination of this text. Again, we can mention only a few things.

No document in the New Testament is written in the abstract. These are not statements made by people simply trying to understand themselves, attempting to get their own heads clear. The communities and individuals responsible for these documents were witnesses to Jesus. The witness was always concrete, specific to a particular context. The letters of Paul differ from one another a great deal because he writes to a wide variety of situations. The situation in Colossae was not the same as that in Galatia, for example, and so Paul's[3] witness to Jesus is not expressed in the same way as it is to the Galatians.

Colossae was located near Ephesus in Asia Minor, in a small triangle of three cities that also included Hieropolis and Laodicea (Col. 4:13). The problem here was not legalism, or "works righteousness," the notion that moral deeds needed to be added to faith in order to gain God's favor. That is the problem Paul addresses in Galatians and also in Romans. The problem in Colossae was Gnosticism, a way of thinking more likely to appear in this place influenced by Greek rather than by Jewish traditions. It was common in the early church, existed in a variety of forms, and can be thought of as a kind of perennial religion with certain affinities to what is now known as New Age religion. Some major cities today even have gnostic bookstores.

Basically, the essential belief behind all varieties of Gnosticism is that reality is split into two realms, the spiritual and the material. Everything works from this basic assumption. Gnosticism comes from the Greek word *gnosis,* which means "knowledge." In this case, the knowledge referred to is secret knowledge that allows the devotee entrance into the spiritual realm, entrance that is not open to ordinary people. So there are secret "philosophies," secret rites and rituals, special days, dates, seasons with significant spiritual importance, secret foods to eat and things to drink, rigid practices to observe. The heavenly bodies were associated with the spiritual realm. A human being also was divided into two parts, an immortal soul that belonged to the spiritual realm, and a mortal body that belonged to the material realm. The soul, or "spirit," was the important part. One could show one's disdain for the body by either subduing it or, on the other hand, just letting it do whatever it wants to do.

The people in the congregation at Colossae were at least tempted toward or influenced by this gnostic dualism. It is clear in Paul's exhortations to them in 2:8 and 2:16-28. They were Christian believers, but their religious ideas were distorting their Christian faith and life. They believed that Jesus Christ was now somehow divine, somehow a god in the spiritual realm, but only one of many beings and powers, rungs on the ladder between our own material existence and God. In this gnostic muddle, Jesus Christ was neither truly human nor truly God.[4]

When Paul addresses them, he does make some very specific exhortations. He warns them not to allow themselves to be deceived (2:8), and enumerates items they should watch out for (2:16-23). But there is no tight argument here against Gnosticism as there is against legalism in Romans and Galatians. What we find is a magnificent doxology in praise to Jesus Christ, who is the center not only of history but of the entire creation. It is a spelling out of what the early confession that Jesus is Lord actually involves. He is Lord of all. Some think Paul is quoting an early hymn. It is true that it is a kind of encapsulated Hallelujah chorus. When the World Council of Churches assembled in New Delhi in 1961 with the theme, "Jesus, the Light of the World," Joseph Sittler gave the keynote address, used this text, and talked about the Cosmic Christ and the Christic Cosmos.[5] The gnostic leanings of the Christians in Colossae led them into a religious partiality. Reality was part spiritual, part material. Jesus Christ was for them partly human, partly divine. Paul proclaims Jesus Christ to them, repeating over and over the words "all things," "everything."

> He is the image of the invisible God, the firstborn of all creation;
> for in him all things in heaven and on earth were created, things
> visible and invisible, whether thrones or dominions or rulers or
> powers—all things have been created through him and for him. He
> himself is before all things, and in him all things hold together. He
> is the head of the body, the church; he is the beginning, the first-
> born from the dead, so that he might have first place in every-
> thing. For in him all the fullness of God was pleased to dwell, and
> through him God was pleased to reconcile to himself all things,

whether on earth or in heaven, by making peace through the
blood of his cross (Col. 1:15-20).

In chapters 3 and 4, Paul begins to work out implications. If this
is what Christian faith is about, what might the Christian life look
like? There are some specifics. Those who know this Jesus will abandon fornication, impurity, evil desire, greed, anger, malice, slander,
abusive language. They will not lie to one another. They will
embrace compassion, kindness, humility, meekness, patience, forgiveness, love. They will be thankful. They will be praying people.
They will make good use of their time. But it is clear that the Christian life is not simply paying attention to a list of specifics. It has to
do with everything one does. There is flexibility. Not every action
can be prescribed in advance. But there is also control, a direction in
which actions are to move. It is stated in 3:17: "And whatever you
do, in word or in deed, do everything in the name of the Lord Jesus."

Calculating consequences in this context and with this perspective is the opposite of the cynicism and egoism that is often implied
when one person refers to another as "a calculating person." Considering the consequences of one's decisions and actions means being
attentive to how one lives one's life in the light of God's purpose in
Jesus Christ for the entire creation. It may sound overwhelming. The
process is helped considerably by the formulating of tentative exceptionless imperatives.

21. The Use of Exceptionless Imperatives

Children, obey your parents in everything. . . . Fathers, do not provoke your children.

—*Colossians* 3:20f.

Consequentialism seeks to formulate exceptionless moral imperatives. These imperatives retain a degree of tentativity, because new information and further reflection may call for adjustment of projected outcomes and reformulation of imperatives.

———

Consequentialism differs from character ethics in that it focuses on conduct rather than character. Character ethicists are interested in conduct, and consequentialists are interested in character, but where the emphasis is placed makes a difference. Character ethicists work primarily with virtues and character traits. Consequentialists work primarily with projected outcomes of decisions and actions.

Consequentialism is also clearly distinguished from situationism. Consequentialism makes decisions and takes actions based on what is calculated to have high degrees of probability to bring about the greatest available good. Situationism makes decisions and takes actions based on what appears, taking everything in the situation into account, to be the most appropriate thing to do. Situationists may well have some interest in consequences, and consequentialists certainly have an interest in details of a given situation. Yet these are two very different ways of understanding morality and of doing ethics.

In the context of the chapter on "Consequentialism and Practical Wisdom," we said that it is deontology with which consequentialism can be most clearly contrasted. This was because both situationism and character ethics can claim to have a major interest in practical wisdom, whereas it would not be an accurate assessment to associate deontology with practical wisdom. In the context of this chapter, having to do with the use of exceptionless imperatives, it is with character ethics and situationism that the contrasts with consequentialism are most striking. Consequentialism and deontology, different as they are in many respects, do in this case exhibit similarities.

The similarities between deontology and consequentialism have to do with the willingness of each to make use of moral rules. These are not simply "rules of thumb" or "cumulative rules" or "presumptive rules," to be set aside whenever the situation demands it, as in situationism. Both deontology and consequentialism are interested in rules that are expected to work for large numbers of people over long periods of time. Deontological rules and consequentialist rules may look similar and in some cases may even be formulated with the same words. The difference lies in how they are derived and how they are regarded.

Let us take, as an example, a rule that states, "You shall not kill." When we talked about deontology, we saw that a deontologist may be interested in putting into words her detailed understanding of this rule. Without such details, there can be no clarity about its meaning. We said that most deontologists would say, to begin, that the rule has to do with human beings. Then different qualifiers would be built into the rule depending on the deontologist's views on self-defense, police action, war, defense of another person, or even defense of one's property. It is clear that no such rule with all qualifications built into it exists in any ideal world out there. Deontologists work very hard to be clear about moral rules. Without such clarity, it would not be possible to talk intelligently about what such rules mean, how they are to be used and applied, what agreements or disagreements about them might exist. What deontologists have in common is the principle of universalizability. They work with rules until they are convinced that the rules can be regarded as universal moral obligations for every person in every time and every place, applicable in every morally relevant case. Morality is, by definition, that which is universally obligatory and applicable.

Consequentialists who work with Christian commitments are likely to be equally attentive to the Ten Commandments, and equally interested in taking the words "You shall not kill" with total seriousness. They also have a great respect for clarity and will want to build details into the rule in order that they themselves, as well as others, will understand what is being said. No two consequentialists are apt to come up with identical qualifications, any more than would two deontologists. The methods are not vending machines and do not produce automatic results. However, let us assume that a given deontologist and a given consequentialist, after a great deal of work, come up with identical rules. They would sound the same, but they would differ in the method by which they were derived, and they would differ in the way they would be regarded.

A deontological rule is derived by asking the question of universalizability, and the rule itself is regarded as a universal moral obligation for every person in every time and every place. The consequentialist rule is very different. It is not derived from the universalizability question, but built up, inductively, from attempts to make sound judgments about probable outcomes of various scenarios. For example, a question when dealing with the injunction not to kill is whether police officers should ever be allowed to use lethal force, and if so, under what conditions. For the consequentialist, this question cannot be approached and certainly not adequately responded to by raising questions concerning universal moral obligations.

A consequentialist might begin with some notions about balances between personal freedom and public safety, realizing that neither is absolute, that both are relative to one another as well as to a multitude of other things. There would be impressions built up from personal experience and reliable studies concerning matters of deterrence, that is, to what extent the mere threat of lethal force by police officers might be expected to deter violent crime. In building up a database, attention would be paid to the source of information. Materials from London in the 1930s would be distinguished from those taken from Chicago in the 1960s and from New York in the 1990s. What kinds of weapons are being used by people committing violent crimes? Ought the public to expect police officers to use pistols to confront criminals using automatic weapons? How do officers in crisis situations evaluate dangers to bystanders in the event of possible crossfire? How volatile are reactions in the community to crimes committed and to various methods used to prevent crimes? How are appropriate proportionalities in the use of police force to be figured out? The only limit on the questions that need to be pursued is the time and energy that can be expended on the problem.

It is possible that a deontologist and a consequentialist may each arrive at the formulation of a rule governing the use of lethal force by police officers, and that the two formulations may be identical. Such a thing is highly unlikely, but it is possible. One difference has to do with the way the rule has been derived. The deontologist will have come to it by asking questions about the universalizability of moral obligations. The consequentialist will have arrived at it inductively via as broad an investigation of data and projected outcomes as it was possible to make. As was indicated in a previous chapter, the consequentialist pursuit of morality integrates empirical data, respects common sense, recognizes human frailty, and embraces probability.

The other major difference lies in how the rule is regarded. A deontological rule, once carefully put together, carries a huge burden of serving as a criterion by which actions are judged to be right or wrong. Although it may be adjusted, it carries tremendous inertia. One does not readily decide to make an adjustment in a universal moral rule. On the other hand, the consequentialist rule is grammatically an exceptionless imperative, but by definition not a universal moral rule. It is a guide for prudent action in circumstances that carry high degrees of moral density. It is designed to work for large numbers of people over long periods of time, but tentativity is built into it. Adjustments and even reformulations on the basis of new data and changes in projected outcomes are not taken lightly, but are nevertheless expected to occur.

The question concerning the use of lethal force by police officers is an example of how the same words in a rule can be derived in different ways and can be regarded in different ways. It makes a difference whether one approaches the commandment, "You shall not kill," in a deontological or in a consequentialist way.

As another example, one could take a brief look at the sentence, "Children, obey your parents in everything" (Col. 3:20). A Christian deontologist is likely to begin with the conviction that this is the right way for children to behave, for every child everywhere to behave. In addition to this rule being clear throughout the Bible, from the Ten Commandments through the writings of Paul, it is the case that no reasonable person could possibly universalize disobedience to parents. No reasonable person could think that a universal moral rule should read, "Children, disobey your parents." As we have seen, details may be built into the rule. It could be observed that a fifty-year-old child need not necessarily obey a seventy-five-year-old parent, especially if that parent is not clear headed. Ages, the character of the parents, whether the parents agree, and whether there are two parents in the home—all kinds of factors may be built into the rule. But, taking such qualifications into account, it is the right thing to do and it is a universal moral obligation.

The Christian consequentialist will also most likely take the sentence, "Children, obey your parents in everything," with great seriousness, and its presence in the Bible will be acknowledged. She will, however, tend to think that the rule is there because it makes a great deal of sense. She is likely to think that a great many people have come to this conclusion over very long periods of time, and that the consequences most likely to be brought about by widespread disobedience to parents would be that social institutions could begin to unravel. The consequentialist may even make observations regarding the state of current society in the United States and may argue that many social ills can be traced to a lack of structure and order in families. On the other hand, there will need to be an adequate recognition of single-parent families, of split and regrouped families, of families with one or even two abusive parents, of irresponsible parents. Important reciprocities need to be taken into account. Other rules, such as, "Fathers, do not provoke your children," may be seen as necessary correlatives without which the first charge to children loses some weight. In any case, the rule, "Children, obey your parents in everything," will be seen as an exceptionless imperative, but not as a universal moral obligation. It will be seen as having been build up inductively, perhaps with many qualifications, and will be regarded as a rule with some tentativity, subject to possible adjustment and perhaps reformulation due to additional information and new projections.

We have said that it is possible that a moral obligation designed to be a deontological rule may read exactly as does an exceptionless imperative put together through a process of considering consequences. The difference would be in how the two emerged and how they are regarded. If in a conversation, the decision needed to be defended, one would know quite quickly who was arguing deontologically and who consequentially. It is also the case, of course, that these two very different ways of understanding morality and of doing ethics may produce quite different results.

Without even trying, one can hear deontological and consequentialist arguments daily in the news, particularly on TV news programs where the format allows for extended questions from the interviewer or interviewers, and on those news talk shows where there are extended exchanges between parties holding different points of view. Some such programs are an insult to the viewer's intelligence. Others are consistently interesting. People who have not thought about or made conscious decisions about the nature of morality and the doing of ethics are not always consistent. But the arguments are there to be heard and analyzed.

The calculation of consequences is very complicated. It requires decisions about whether the degree of moral density in the matter warrants the effort of considering the consequences. It requires some attempt at risk/benefit analysis, making use of alternative scenarios. It has no choice but to make educated guesses, to take calculated risks, to work with probabilities in the context of uncertainties. It must build in feedback devices in order to monitor the movement toward the goal and in order to make mid-course corrections when necessary. In addition to prayer and conversation with others whose counsel is respected, Christian consequentialists need to read the Bible carefully to understand as clearly as possible the text in its context then and there, in order to do as serious a job as possible to recontextualize that text in the here and now. That requires knowing something about the present context as well as knowing something about the context of the biblical document being read. Understanding morality and doing ethics in a consequentialist way is extremely complicated.

On the other hand, morality is an important social institution, essential for the sustaining and flourishing of human life, and of ecosystems on which human life depends. In matters with high degrees of moral density, it is worth the effort. Furthermore, the process is not so strange. It involves practical wisdom that we use daily in many areas of life, formally and informally. There is accumulated wisdom of the past on which to draw and empirical data and common sense to which attention should be paid. There are some shared hopes and some relatively common notions about what might constitute the common good. The human mind is an amazing piece of God's creation. When used conscientiously, it is capable of doing well even with extremely complicated tasks.

Of considerable help in this process is the willingness to formulate and make use of exceptionless imperatives that can serve, at least tentatively, as guides for more specific decisions and actions. Such exceptionless imperatives are designed with the thought that they may be useful to large numbers of people over long periods of time. But they are not "absolute." They remain open to adjustment and even reformulation as new data appear and different projections are made.

Afterword ~

Christian Faith and Moral Behavior: Connections

22. Believing and Behaving

Therefore, be imitators of God.
—The author of the letter to the Ephesians

Although there is no single straight line from Christian faith to .
specific and detailed moral behaviors, there are and should be
connections between believing and behaving.

~~~

In the Foreword, it was important to establish disjunctions between
moral behavior and Christian faith. This was done by demonstrating
that the two terms are not interchangeable, by asserting that interest
in morality and ethics far exceeds interest in Christianity, and by
exploring difficulties that arise when the term "Christian Ethics" is
used. The importance of recognizing these disjunctions, it was stated,
is that genuine conversation among Christians about moral disputes
cannot proceed if these disjunctions are ignored.

At this point we turn to a statement about connections between
Christian faith and moral behavior. To assure that the disjunctions in
the Foreword would not be misunderstood as a complete separation
of faith from life, or confession from conduct, it was stated there
clearly that there are connections. There were a few references to
statements from Jesus and John, Martin Luther and Dietrich Bonhoeffer. In fact, the entire Christian tradition insists that there are,
and should be, connections between Christian faith and moral
behavior, between believing and behaving. The point is made in
many different ways.

One can make a case, for example, that there exists in the Bible a
pattern that moves from a presentation of Christian belief to a presentation of some implications of that belief for Christian behavior.

This pattern is not present everywhere in the Bible, and it is not essential to the claim that there are connections between believing and behaving. Yet there are striking examples of this pattern, and many readers of the Bible have noticed them.

The first three chapters of Ephesians are a verbal symphony of praise to the cosmic drama of the God of creation and redemption working through Jesus the crucified and risen Lord to accomplish God's purpose for all things and all peoples. There follows a distinct pause, after which the reader can almost hear the wild applause. Then comes the unmistakable "Therefore." Since this is what God has done and is doing and will do, and since God has called you into the fellowship of believers, it follows that you should "lead a life worthy of the calling to which you have been called" (Eph. 4:1). The connection drawn between believing and behaving is decisive and dramatic. This pattern is repeated in specific passages in Ephesians. It is unmistakable. "And be kind to one another, tenderhearted, forgiving one another, as God in Christ has forgiven you. Therefore be imitators of God, as beloved children, and live in love, as Christ loved us" (Eph. 4:32–5:2). Thomas à Kempis wrote about *The Imitation of Christ*. The more daring author of this letter to the congregation at Ephesus says that believers are to imitate the behavior of God.

A careful reader of the Bible who noticed this pattern and recognized that the pattern has everything to do with ways Christians can think about morality and ethics was the Lutheran theologian Joseph Sittler. He devoted an entire book to it, *The Structure of Christian Ethics*.[1] His introductory chapter is titled "The Confusion in Contemporary Ethical Speech." He talks about the "organic" nature of biblical language, indicating that the initiative of God and the human response to that initiative are of one piece. This is then explicated in the next two chapters, "The Shape of the Engendering Deed" and "The Content of the Engendered Response." In this recently republished book, Sittler captures beautifully the pattern about which we are speaking.

What was seen to be the case in Ephesians, and what Sittler saw as a basic biblical pattern, is true in other New Testament documents. In Romans, Paul spends eleven chapters in a powerful, sometimes very tightly argued, rejection of the idea that good works must be added to faith to gain God's favor. Having driven home that point about believing, he moves in chapter 12 to implications of that believing for behaving. "I appeal to you therefore, brothers and sisters, to present your bodies as a living sacrifice, holy and acceptable to God, which is your spiritual worship" (Rom.12:1). In Colossians, as we have seen, the fact that God does everything in, through, and for Jesus (Col. 1:15-20) moves to the fact that we should do everything we do in the name of Jesus (Col. 3:17). The pattern is carried out in other ways. The indicative of God's initiative is tied very closely to the imperative of human response: "You have died. . . . Therefore, put to death" (Col. 3:3-5).

The pattern is there even in the Sermon on the Mount (Matt. 5:1–7:28). This section, often read as the moral teaching of Jesus, is actually focused on Jesus himself. The centerpiece is 5:17-20, in which Jesus is proclaimed to be the fulfillment of the Law and the Prophets. The word "fulfill" is used eleven times in Matthew to drive home this fact, which is Matthew's central message. The actions referred to in the Sermon on the Mount are indicative of the way followers of Jesus find themselves behaving. This is why the Sermon on the Mount (and also the "Sermon on the Plain" in Luke) begin by calling these followers "blessed," even "happy," as the NRSV has it. The verb *essesthe* in 5:48 translated as an imperative *"Be perfect"* is an ambiguous form in Greek. It is translated as a present imperative, but can, and would more appropriately, be translated as future indicative. It would then read, *"You will be perfect."* Seeing that God has the initiative, and placing Jesus in the center, makes a great deal of difference. It is not a demand that we be morally perfect, but rather a promise that, when we follow Jesus, God will perfect us, will bring us to be that which God intends us to be.

There are, of course, many places where the pattern is packed into a very short space. "Beloved, since God loved us so much, we also ought to love one another" (1 John 4:11). Even the Ten Commandments, often taken to be simple commands about human behavior, are first and primarily a declaration about God's prior redemptive act. What is unfortunately left out in Luther's Small Catechism is the all important preface, "I am the LORD your God who brought you out of the land of Egypt" (Exod. 20:2). Only following that declaration come the exhortations. Again, it is the move from God's initiative to human response that is the hinge on which the whole thing swings.

An impressive case can be made for saying that there is a pattern discernible in the Bible, one that moves from believing to behaving, from confession to conduct, from the Good News about Jesus to the new life in Christ. There are, and there ought to be, connections between believing and behaving. We mentioned early in this chapter that Joseph Sittler noticed it and expressed it beautifully in his work. It has seemed an obvious pattern to others also. C. H. Dodd, the great Oxford New Testament scholar, talked about it as the move from *kerygma* to *didache* in his pivotal work, *The Apostolic Preaching and Its Developments*.[2] Later he worked through the same pattern in a more thorough and systematic way in his book *Gospel and Law*.[3] Lutheran poet Gerhard Frost used to express it by saying, "Deep in the heart of love, there beats an 'ought.'"

Karl Barth was a systematic theologian. But, as any good Christian theologian does, he worked constantly with biblical texts. He saw the pattern clearly, and it developed in many ways in his writings. The very early Barth wrote a commentary on Romans, which catapulted him from the village church in Safenwil, Switzerland, to the University of Bonn in Germany. It was a purely existentialist treatment of Paul, very similar to the kind of work that Bultmann did throughout his life. The ethical implications were purely situational. But Barth soon moved to a more linear way of understanding God's involvement in history, and the pattern of moving from God's initiative to human response became clear.

We already pointed to this in the Foreword, when talking about problems that arise when the term "Christian Ethics" is used. In order to be clear that Christian behavior follows Christian believing, in the *Church Dogmatics* Barth first laid out a doctrine, then those ethical implications that flowed from it. There are three separate books on the Doctrine of Creation (III/1, III/2, III/3). Only then does Barth come with III/4, which he titles *Ethics as a Task of the Doctrine of Creation*. He explicated the pattern specifically in an article entitled "Gospel and Law."[4]

In his book *The Humanity of God*, Barth makes the same point.[5] The God of the Bible is best known in the flesh of Jesus of Nazareth. Therefore, if we want to know what it is to be human, we look first to the humanity of God in Jesus. From him we learn what it means to live our own lives as human. When working with Romans 5:12-21, Paul's treatment of God's action in Christ to deal with the sin brought into creation by Adam, Barth titles his book as one would expect, *Christ and Adam*.[6] The order is significant. When Barth talks about the creedal affirmation, "He ascended into heaven and is seated at the right hand of God, the Father Almighty," he says it is not that we have hands, and then project our own ideas into heaven in order to understand God. It is exactly the opposite. God has hands. God is the maker, the creator. God formed us with God's own hands from the dust of the earth (Gen. 2:7). When we understand what it means that God has hands, then we shall be ready to begin to understand what it means that we have hands, and to think clearly about how to use them creatively.[7]

The Lutheran Joseph Sittler, the Calvinist Karl Barth, the Congregationalist C. H. Dodd, and a great many others have detected a pattern in the Bible that moves from God's initiative to human response, from confession to conduct, from covenant to command, from believing to behaving, from the Good News about Jesus to the new life in Christ, from Gospel to Law. Every Christian knows that there are, and should be, connections between Christian faith and moral behavior. That much is crystal clear. Not every Christian understands those connections in terms of the pattern we have been describing.

Many Lutherans, for example, while not denying that such a pattern exists many places in the Bible, insist that theologically it is absolutely essential to speak of "Law and Gospel" rather than of "Gospel and Law." The position has a great deal to do with the argument of Paul in Romans and Galatians against legalism and "works righteousness." Against a gross misunderstanding of the law that treats it as a way to gain God's favor, Paul says the law only serves to show us that we cannot by good works of the law be justified by God. God declares us justified, or righteous, only "by faith" (Rom. 1:17). Luther found his own experience described precisely and powerfully by Paul, and built his own theology around the "Justification by Faith" theme. Controversies and debates over these matters have raged at least since the sixteenth-century Reformation. Lutheran theologian Dietrich Bonhoeffer decided it was necessary to say it both ways, "Law and Gospel" and "Gospel and Law." It is an important conversation among serious theologians. What is not in doubt is that there are, and should be, connections between believing and behaving.

We have emphasized the biblical pattern that seems to be most generic in the Christian tradition, and most helpful in understanding the relationship between Christian faith and moral behavior. Variations on the theme of connections between these two are, however, almost endless. Since all Christians make some connection, it is done in simple and informal ways as well as in the context of formal theological analysis and reflection.

One popular way in which the connection has been acknowledged is by the wearing of "WWJD" bracelets. The letters stand for "What would Jesus do?" and the idea is that those who believe in Jesus should seek guidance for their behavior by asking, whenever in doubt, what Jesus would do. It is a way of connecting believing and behaving, and that much can be commended. It may even serve to help the wearer to be conscious and conscientious about keeping Jesus in mind when making important decisions. Beyond that, it is difficult to imagine how "WWJD" is of any concrete help in understanding morality or in doing ethics. The move from WWJD to an important decision is simply too big a jump.

Among the multitudes of studies concerning how the connections between believing and behaving have been understood in the life of the church, there are a few classics. One, previously mentioned here, that has been in print for a long time and has been read by many thousands is *Christ and Culture*[8] by H. Richard Niebuhr, who taught Christian Ethics at Yale and trained many ethicists still working in the field. The work has not been without its critics.[9] Yet whatever its shortcomings, it has served many as an extremely useful tool. Niebuhr asks of the Bible and of the entire Christian tradition how the relation between Christ and culture is to be understood. He finds five major groupings that he believes can be traced throughout the centuries. They are: "Christ against culture," "Christ of culture," "Christ above culture," "Christ and culture in paradox," "Christ the transformer of culture." Although Niebuhr finds himself in the final category, he correctly sees all of these as possible ways to make the connections.

Not as well known, but also a great classic study, is *Christ and the Moral Life* by James Gustafson.[10] It has also already been mentioned. The question Gustafson asks is very carefully crafted. He wants to study "some of the differences that faith in Jesus Christ *often does make, can make,* and *ought to make* in the moral lives of members of the

Christian community."[11] It is, very specifically, a question about
connections between believing and behaving. The work is similar to
that of Niebuhr, in that Gustafson works through the New Testament and the entire history of the church. It is different in that
Gustafson sees key figures such as Luther, Calvin, Barth, and Bonhoeffer, all expressing themselves in a number of different ways.
Thus many appear in more than one of his major descriptions.
Gustafson thinks the relationship has been understood and expressed
in five ways: "Jesus Christ, the Lord who is Creator and Redeemer,"
"Jesus Christ, the Sanctifier," "Jesus Christ, the Justifier," "Jesus
Christ, the Pattern," and "Jesus Christ, the Teacher."

When one reads the Bible with care and examines the history of
serious reflection in the church, it is clear that there is no single
straight line from Christian faith to moral behavior. It is also clear,
however, that there are—and should be—connections between
believing and behaving.

Afterword⟶

23. Moral Directions and Action Directives

If we really want to live, we'd better start at once to try.
If we don't, it doesn't matter, but we'd better start to die.
—*W. H. Auden*

As connections are worked out between believing and behaving, it is helpful to distinguish broad moral directions from more specific action directives.

⟶ ⟵

It should be clear at this point that when the term "moral directions" is used in this book, it does not refer to one person telling another, "Do this! Do that!" The word "direction" means pointing somewhere, moving toward a goal, aiming to accomplish something, having a purpose in mind. To live with direction is the opposite of Ibsen's Peer Gynt, who sits and peels the onion only to find that there is no center, no core, that everything is only wrappings. It is the opposite of concluding that "all is vanity" (Eccles. 1:2), that life is nothing but emptiness. Moral life is here taken to be, by definition, life with a purpose, life that moves consciously and conscientiously toward a goal, in the direction of a desired and anticipated end. The integrity of the moral life comes from this purposefulness. It is what some call a seamless life.

We have attempted to explore how an ethical methodology could be worked out in the context of Christian commitments by considering consequentialism. It is clear that it is a teleological method, one that understands morality and does ethics on the basis of probabilities of projected outcomes. The calculation of consequences requires moving one's mind and heart in a forward direction. The entire project is taken to be congruent with the whole message of the whole Bible, which describes the forward movement of the living God from the creation on toward the redemption of all things. Both

149

Platonic and Kantian Idealism are rejected, along with that gnostic dualism that plagued the Christians in Colossae. Aristotle's interest in the *telos* is taken to be congenial to but certainly not identical to the *eschaton* of the New Testament and to that eschatological hope that feeds back into the minds and hearts of expectant believers. It means moving in the direction that God is moving, toward the goal that God has in mind. It means, in fact, nothing less than "imitating God" (Eph. 5:1).

It should also be clear that we are not talking about just any purpose in life. We are talking about moving in the direction of God's purpose in Jesus Christ for the entire creation. Both Adolf Hitler and Mother Teresa lived their lives with a purpose in mind. Hitler's purpose was evil, demonic, against what God has in mind. And the means by which he sought to carry out that purpose were destructive of everything God wants done in this world. Mother Teresa lived attempting to do something beautiful for God and found gracious ways to do it. It would be a massive misunderstanding of what is being said here were someone to conclude that any purpose, any goal, will do.

Ibsen's Peer Gynt has no purpose at all. Ibsen's Brand has a misguided purpose. He is single minded but also simple minded. He gets into his head what God wants him to do and then never pauses to check it, never reflects on whether he has heard correctly, whether things are going badly. He is a zealot, leaving nothing but destruction and death in his path. Only at the end of the last scene when he is being buried by an avalanche and he calls out asking how a person can be redeemed, does he finally hear a voice, "He is the God of Love." A useful exercise would be to read Ibsen's *Brand* and Kierkegaard's *Purity of Heart Is to Will One Thing* in conjunction with one another. Not just any purpose will do.

We have frequently talked about God's purpose in terms of "redemption," of bringing back to God's self that which has been in bondage to sin, to forces moving against God. The description of God's purpose in the Bible is, of course, magnificently rich. It is to reconcile that which is alienated; to atone, to make at one that which has disintegrated; to adopt those who have been orphaned, those who are alone; to save that which is lost; to sanctify that which is smudged and tawdry. God's purpose is to make old things new, to turn misdirected people around, to forgive and to forget wrongs done with malice or thoughtlessness, to love the unlovely and the unlovable, to treat as "righteous" those who are not. God's purpose is that those who are at war with one another will live together in peace, that those who treat one another unjustly will practice justice, that those who behave toward one another in unkind ways will become considerate of one another.

The great diversity in the biblical description of God's purpose is mirrored in the numerous titles assigned to Jesus. He is not only the Christ. He is Lord, Savior, Redeemer, the Way, the Truth, the Life. He is mediator of the new covenant, an example in suffering, the lamb slain from the foundation of the world. He is door, shepherd, vine. There is only one incarnate, crucified, and risen Jesus, as there is one triune God and one creation. The ways in which the Bible describes the end toward which everything is moving is wonderfully diverse. The purpose of God is magnificently rich. Learning to feel and love its texture takes more than a lifetime of growth and maturation. It is why Christian parents begin the day their children are born to point them in the right direction, the direction of God's purpose. They begin to do it by whispering the name of Jesus into their ears.

This entire conceptualization will sound quite natural and normal to many people who see it as analogous to the way they attempt to live their lives. They try to make prudent decisions, to take whatever calculated risks seem to be necessary and reasonable, to make what use they can of what they consider to be practical wisdom. They not only think they ought to be kind, to tell the truth, to keep promises. They think it makes a great deal of sense to do so. They believe that things are more likely to go well when people behave in these ways. Some who find this conceptualization congenial will be Christians, and they will see this way of talking about Christian faith and life as a fairly accurate and not at all surprising description of what the Bible and Christianity are basically about. On the other hand, some will see this entire way of understanding morality and of doing ethics as, at the very least, strange. If they are Christians, they may think it quite different from what they have thought the Christian faith and life to be about.

To understand these two responses, it may be helpful to take a brief look at the work of Dietrich Bonhoeffer, whom we have already mentioned a number of times. He was a thoroughly Christocentric

person and theologian. He was a Christian and knew that God is triune. He also knew that the doctrine of the triune God developed in
the church as it began to spell out implications of its conviction that
Jesus Christ is truly God and truly human. Taking with total seriousness the fact that the God of the Bible is best known in the flesh
of Jesus of Nazareth drove Bonhoeffer to reject what he called "two-
sphere thinking."[1] He used the term to refer to the separation of reality into two spheres, the spiritual and the material, the timeless and
the temporal, the soul and the body, God and the world. He saw this
two-sphere thinking to be characteristic of much religious thought,
even much religious thought among Christians. He therefore struggled with what rejecting this two-sphere thinking would mean for
Christianity, what Christianity "without religion" would look like.
In his letters from prison to his friend Eberhard Bethge, he began to
talk about "religionless Christianity," "this-worldly transcendence,"
"holy worldliness," "God in the midst of life."

Bonhoeffer saw that the Christian claim is that there are not two
spheres separated from one another, but one reality that is God and
world together in Jesus Christ. It is not strange that he loved to
quote from Colossians. He saw God and world together in motion
toward the achievement of God's purpose, and he saw that the appropriate response of the Christian was to get in on this and to take
responsibility for shaping the future according to God's purpose.[2] It
was a teleological way of doing Christian theology and ethics.
Because Bonhoeffer knew that those who thought of Christian faith
and life in terms of "two-sphere thinking" would find his rejection of
it strange, he faced that fact squarely and said it plainly:

> Whoever wishes to take up the problem of a Christian ethic must
> be confronted at once with a demand which is quite without par-
> allel. He must from the outset discard as irrelevant the two ques-
> tions which alone impel him to concern himself with the problem
> of ethics, "How can I be good?" and "How can I do good?", and
> instead of these he must ask the utterly and totally different ques-
> tion "What is the will of God?"[3]

"The will of God" is not an empty phrase. Nor is it a brief ecstatic
revelation to a lonely individual. It has to do with the future of God's
creation, with the redemptive purpose of the Creator for all things
and all peoples, with the behavior of those who believe, the conduct

of those who confess, the purposeful lives of those who proclaim the purpose of God. Since God is not motionless, the will of God for us is not static. It is not, therefore, best described in timeless principles or ideals or rules, but rather in dynamic directions. God's will for us is that we choose life, rather than death, so that we and our descendants may live (Deut. 30:19). It is that we move according to God's purpose and make that purpose our own.

Consequentialists formulate exceptionless imperatives designed to be useful to large numbers of people over long periods of time. When very broad, they can be called "moral directions." They are not deontologically constructed universal moral obligations. One way in which Kant formulated "the categorical imperative" was: "So act so that you can will your action as a universal law for all humankind." The formulation is based on the principle of universalizability. One way a Christian consequentialist might formulate a moral direction could be, "So act so that your action is designed to work with, rather than against, the purpose of God." The focus is not on universalizability, but on directionality. An example of such a rule in the Bible, already mentioned, would be, "Whatever you do, in word or in deed, do everything in the name of the Lord Jesus." It is not an empty phrase. As we have seen, it has to do with the future of God's creation. The Christian is one who lives with a purpose, and that purpose is to "do the will of God," that is, to seek to allow God to use one's actions to facilitate, rather than to frustrate, God's redemptive purpose for all things. In the words of Joseph Sittler, it is to allow "the content of the engendered response" to be informed by and filled in conformity to "the shape of the engendering deed." In the words of the author to the Ephesians, it is to "imitate God."

It is possible that one might have difficulty finding a Christian consequentialist who would disagree with this very broad moral direction for Christian behavior. The more specific one gets, the greater the likelihood that opinions will begin to diverge. Christians who make connections between the creation and the Creator have every reason to care for the environment and to see this activity as moving along with God's will and purpose.[4] Greater specificity often brings greater divergence. One person might formulate her conviction by saying, "Always act so that your action will contribute to the preservation and flourishing of the creation, whether or not it places the human race in jeopardy." Another may say, "Always act so that your action will contribute to the preservation and future flourishing of the creation, attempting at the same time to avoid placing the human race in jeopardy." These two agree on a basic formulation of a moral direction. As they get more specific, they find important ways in which they begin to diverge. It will not be a surprise if they find themselves in total disagreement when they get to very specific issues, such as how to manage logging in the Pacific Northwest or whether to explore possible offshore oil reserves. When it gets to action directives—what to do in a specific case—conversation partners will do well occasionally to move back toward moral directions to check what it is they may have in common. On the way back to the action directives, there may be greater understanding of one another's position.

Two Christian consequentialists may be in total agreement that the family is not a human invention, but a way that God has ordained to order the creation and to preserve human life. They may agree on a moral direction that could read, "So act that your action serves to promote God's purpose to preserve the family as a fundamental social institution, never to move in the direction of destroying or even diminishing it." It is not an empty statement. There are heavy commitments in the formulation. It is a moral direction. Two Christian consequentialists may agree on it. It is likely, however, that as they move closer to more specific action directives, their opinions may begin to diverge. Long before getting into a verbal war about sex education in public schools, or cohabitation, or insurance for domestic partners, there could be a pause and a return to a shared conviction about a moral direction. Having reminded one another that they have the same goal in mind, they may be able to move again, more cautiously, toward constructive conversation about more specific action directives. This time there might be more careful reflection and explanation of why chosen means are thought likely to bring about desired ends.

The distinction between broad and specific need not apply only to consequentialists. It certainly can apply to conversation between or with deontologists. It may even serve well for those situationists who want to work with rather large "cumulative rules" or "presumptive rules." Thomas Aquinas, working with Natural Law reflections on how to understand congruences between Creator and creation, knew very well that it was necessary to acknowledge gradations when formulating moral obligations. He writes:

> The more you descend into the detail the more it appears how the general rule admits of exceptions, so that you have to hedge it with cautions and qualifications. The greater the number of conditions accumulated the greater the number of ways in which the principle is seen to fall short. . . .[5]

It is a very common sense reality, yet often ignored by people in the heat of moral disputes, that it is important to distinguish between broad moral directions and specific action directives. If they know where they are on a graduated scale between the two, they can move back and forth as they clarify and explain. It is possible to imagine a grid with gradations between moral directions and action directives on one axis, and degrees of moral density on the other. The process itself of discussing where the subject of the conversation might be located on the grid could be instrumental in furthering understanding of positions. There would inevitably be talk about alternative means to reach chosen ends.

Talk about sliding scales from high to low degrees of moral density and from very broad moral directions to very specific action directives will sound to some like an invitation to moral relativism. It is true that it is a departure from the moral absolutes of many deontological positions. But in the context of serious Christian commitments to move in the direction of God's purpose in Jesus Christ for the entire creation, it is anything but arbitrary. People who can agree on a moral direction ought at least to be able to converse about the action directives that may be necessary to follow in order to move in that direction. And that may help in the difficult task of ordering civil conversation about serious moral disagreements.

Afterword ⟶

24. Civil Conversation about Serious Disagreements

Of all the lost arts—the stained glass of Chartres, the tiles of Delft, the ink of Gutenberg, the memory system of the Renaissance, the singing of the cas-trati, the speech of the ancient Romans, the poetry of the minnesingers, illu-minated manuscripts, Gobelin tapestry . . . the most lamented is the art of conversation.
    —Robert Darnton, The New York Review of Books

The fact that we share a mutually dependent and precarious future, in which the consequences of our believing and behav-ing are increasingly significant, ought to make clear the impor-tance of civil conversation about serious moral disagreements.

⟶〜⟵

This is a book about Christian Ethics. It is not a book, however, about conclusions that the author has reached on various moral quandaries. It is rather a book about how people tend to reach con-clusions on what they consider to be moral matters. A consistent theme throughout has been that whatever else ethics is, it is a set of methods and mechanisms that can help to bring into civil and con-structive conversation people with significant moral disagreements. If some people are helped along the way toward such conversation, the book will have served its purpose.

Conversation is not the goal of morality. The goal of the institu-tion of morality is the health and flourishing of the human race and of the entire creation with its interlaced ecosystems without which life would be impossible. Almost everyone agrees that moral behav-ior is of great consequence, but there is a great deal of disagreement about how to respond to moral questions, and even about what con-stitutes morality. Civil conversation about these disagreements is the only alternative to the use of force, whether that force is clever rhetoric or street demonstrations, the ballot box or violence. Some use of force may at times be necessary, but it is surely preferable, whenever possible, to give conversation a chance to achieve at least an understanding of why others think as they do. If this is going to happen, conversation partners must know not only what they think, but why they think as they do.

Recognizing that there are both disjunctions and connections between believing and behaving ought to help. Recognizing that morality is a social institution in which all people have some interest, and that ethics is a discipline in which almost everyone has something to learn from almost everyone else ought to help. Recognizing the precarious existence that we all share on this planet and the high stakes of moral decisions ought to help.

The epigraph with which this chapter begins is from the opening paragraph of a review by Robert Darnton of *The Sense of Reality: Studies in Ideas and Their History* by Sir Isaiah Berlin. Darnton praises Berlin by saying that he is the last of the line of conversationalists and perhaps the greatest of them all. "He has been everywhere, met everyone, read everything." And yet, Berlin has not written as one telling another what to think or to do. He has written inviting his reader to converse with him, to question, to offer alternatives. "Berlin speaks to us, his readers, without a hint of condescension. He draws us into the discussion and infects us with his energy." So many have learned so much from Isaiah Berlin because he knew, above all, the wonder and the preciousness of genuine conversation about important matters.[1]

Civil conversation about serious moral disagreements is only possible when those who have worked hard to come to disagreement continue to work hard at opportunities for further conversation. The following are a few suggestions. It is a random list. Readers will want to add some that they have found helpful.

1. Assume during the conversation that those who disagree with you are just as committed to the task as you are. Assume also that they are just as sensitive, just as compassionate and caring, just as informed. Assume that the person who disagrees with you is your moral equal and that your disagreement is genuine and about matters of substance.

2. Pay attention to and respond to the content of comments from others. Do not divert or short circuit the conversation by turning it into a series of observations or accusations about the person with

whom you are talking. Comments like "You can't understand because you don't live where I live" or "You're really defensive" seldom move a conversation forward.

3. Use clear, clean, and neutral language as much as possible. Opinions should be presented as opinions, not as indisputable facts. Avoid slogans. For example, if you want to converse about disagreements regarding abortion, avoid slogans such as "pro-life" and "pro-choice" or phrases such as "killing unborn babies" and "violating women's reproductive rights." Such things may serve effectively on banners in demonstrations, but they hinder rather than promote conversation.

4. Try to begin with clarity about what the point of contention actually is. Frequently, there is a great deal on which disputants agree. It is helpful to get such things on the table, whether these are moral directions, principles, values, moral rules, or facts related to the matter at hand. Careful work is impossible unless the point of contention is clearly defined.

5. Recognize that words seldom have entirely obvious or universal meanings. People function not only with different ideas of right and wrong, but also different ideas of what "right" and "wrong" mean. The same is true about words like morality, justice, rights, love, freedom. Don't assume that everyone works with your definitions. Find out how others use the words on which the conversation turns.

6. Realize that moral issues are often highly charged emotionally and that there is a strong tendency to generalize on one's own experience. If emotional outbursts occur, try to remain calm and sympathetic. It may take a great deal of patience and generosity. Responding in kind will almost surely bring the conversation quickly to an unhappy end.

7. Give reasons for your opinions that the one with whom you are speaking will find at least interesting. Appeals to raw authority, conscience, or to highly personal experiences are seldom of any help.

8. Exercise courtesy. It is a common human virtue. It is a minimum requirement for constructive conversation about controversial matters. Work with an understanding of the Golden Rule that might read: "Be as courteous to the one who disagrees with you as you would have that person be to you."[2]

Finally, it may be appropriate to suggest a definition of Christian Ethics. What is offered is merely an attempt to be generic, to define in such a way that others doing ethics in a Christian context will at least recognize elements that they also think should be incorporated into such a definition. There are biases, but an attempt has been made to keep them at a minimum.

The author's working definition goes like this: Christian Ethics is a theological discipline by which the church seeks to formulate criteria for living (both personal and corporate, both character and conduct) in the context of the Scriptures and the tradition, but also of the wisdom of the past, the examination of the present, and the planning of the future.

A few comments may be in order concerning key words in the definition. The word *Christian* used together with the word *ethics* raises many questions that have been responded to in many ways. It is a *theological* discipline because the Christian doing ethics must remember at all times that she is indeed a Christian, and that twenty centuries of Christian reflection on the content of the Christian faith are available as materials feeding into the working out of implications for moral behavior. It is a *discipline* both in the sense that it is an academic discipline that can be taught and learned, and in the sense that it is not just a body of information, but a skill, something that one learns to do.

It is something that the *church* does. Because Christianity is intrinsically corporate rather than individualistic, anyone wishing to do it must do it in the awareness that she is one member of the many-membered Body of Christ. It means paying attention to, and taking into consideration, that which other members of the Body have thought and done, and what they are thinking and doing. The church is always a pilgrim people, on the way, moving forward, thus always *seeking* to get its work done. When one day's work ends, the work of the next day begins. The task of Christian Ethics is in motion because God is at work, Jesus is alive, the Holy Spirit is moving.

Ethical criteria in Christian perspective are not simply discovered or simply received. They are *formulated* as a response by moral agents to the prior initiative of God. Formulated *criteria* may be values or virtues, rules, descriptions of appropriate actions, goals or projected ends, moral directions or action directives, depending on what one thinks morality is about and how ethical reflection is being done. In any case, morality has to do with the total person engaged in the totality of *life*. There are degrees of moral density, but nothing is absolutely devoid of moral content. *Personal* and *social* life are distinguishable, but inseparable, as are *character* and *conduct*.

Because Christians know God through the marks of God's involvement in human history, Christian theology and ethics must be done in the *context* of these historic events. The Christian *Scriptures* are the record, the communal memory, of those among whom God has specifically acted. It is the primary source for doing Christian Ethics. The suggestion here is that serious work with biblical materials involves an attempt to recontextualize in the here and now the text that was contextualized in the there and then. The Bible is itself *tradition*. It is *paradosis,* that which was handed down through the gathered community. This handing down continues, as the church lives on, in creeds and confessional statements that arise at times when great issues, such as the person and work of Jesus Christ, are at risk. These documents are important records of the church's reflection on the Christian faith and life and thus indispensable resources for Christians who do ethics.

There is much to be learned from the cumulative *wisdom of the past*. Sorting out lessons from history is complex and controversial, but there can be no excuse for ignoring history. The present cannot be equated with the past. *The present must be examined* and observed as closely as possible to determine what data are available with which to work. Christians do not just plan for the future, as though whatever will be will be, and our only task is to be ready for whatever comes. Christians engage in the *planning of the future*. They take their responsibility as moral agents seriously, knowing that the consequences of their actions will affect not only their own lives, but the lives of many others.

And whatever you do, in word or deed, do everything in the name of the Lord Jesus.

Notes

Foreword—1. Behaving and Believing

1. Tertullian, *Apology,* trans. T. R. Glover (London: Heinemann; New York: G. P. Putnam's, 1931), 177.

2. Martin Luther, *Works of Martin Luther,* vol. 6 (Philadelphia: Muhlenberg, 1932), 451.

3. Dietrich Bonhoeffer, *The Cost of Discipleship*, trans. R. H. Fuller (New York: Macmillan, 1949), 38.

4. Jerry Bock, Jerome Robbins, Joseph Stein, and Sheldon Narnick, *Fiddler on the Roof* (New York: Limelight Publications, 1990).

5. See Karl Rahner, *Theological Investigations,* vol. 13, trans. D. Bourke (New York: Seabury, 1975), 158.

6. Dietrich Bonhoeffer, *Letters and Papers from Prison,* ed. E. Bethge (New York: Macmillan, 1972), 373. This passage is from the letter of 27 July 1944.

Foreword—2. Morality, Humanity, and Christianity

1. Jeffrey Stout, *Ethics after Babel: The Languages of Morals and Their Discontents* (Boston: Beacon, 1988).

2. Saint Augustine, *Confessions,* trans. R. S. Pine-Coffin (New York: Penguin, 1961), 21.

3. Friedrich Schleiermacher, *The Christian Faith in Outline,* trans. D. M. Baillie (Edinburgh: Henderson, 1922), 6.

4. Paul Tillich, *Systematic Theology,* vol. 1 (London: Nisbet, 1953), 14.

5. John B. Cobb Jr., *Christ in a Pluralistic Age* (Philadelphia: Westminster, 1975).

Foreword—3. Questions about Christian Ethics

1. This appears in the appendix of the German biography by Eberhard Bethge, *Dietrich Bonhoeffer* (Munich: Kaiser Verlag, 1967), 1073.

2. Dietrich Bonhoeffer, *Ethics,* ed. E. Bethge, trans. N. H. Smith (New York: Macmillan, 1965).

3. James M. Gustafson, *Can Ethics be Christian?* (Chicago: University of Chicago Press, 1977).

4. James M. Gustafson, *Christ and the Moral Life* (New York: Harper, 1968).

5. James M. Gustafson, *Ethics from a Theocentric Perspective*, vols. 1 and 2 (Chicago: University of Chicago Press, 1983, 1992).

6. Joseph Fletcher, *Situation Ethics* (Louisville: Westminster John Knox, 1997), 60.

7. Ramsey's very sharp critique of Fletcher can be found in chapter 7, "The Case of Joseph Fletcher and Joseph Fletcher's Cases," in Paul Ramsey, *Deeds and Rules in Christian Ethics* (New York: Scribner's, 1967).

4. Morality as Social Institution

1. For valuable discussions of this question, see H. Tristam Engelhardt Jr., *Bioethics and Secular Humanism: The Search for a Common Humanity* (Philadelphia: Trinity, 1991), and Gene Outka and John P. Reeder Jr., eds., *Prospects for a Common Morality* (Princeton: Princeton University Press, 1993).

2. The psychiatrist M. Scott Peck seems to suggest that there are those who are simply evil. See M. Scott Peck, *People of the Lie: The Hope for Healing Human Evil* (New York: Simon and Schuster, 1983).

3. It was a distinct contribution of the Social Gospel Movement that it recognized the extent to which sin penetrates social structures. See Walter Rauschenbusch, *A Theology for the Social Gospel* (New York: Macmillan, 1918).

4. Reinhold Niebuhr, *Moral Man and Immoral Society: A Study in Ethics and Politics* (New York: Scribner's, 1960).

5. Oliver O'Donovan, *Resurrection and Moral Order: An Outline for Evangelical Ethics*, 2d ed. (Grand Rapids: Eerdmans, 1994). For another discussion of this question, see Nancey Murphy and George F. R. Ellis, *On the Moral Nature of the Universe: Theology, Cosmology, and Ethics* (Minneapolis: Fortress, 1996).

6. James Gustafson, *Ethics from a Theocentric Perspective*, vol. 1, reprint (Chicago: University of Chicago Press, 1983).

7. Tom L. Beauchamp, *Philosophical Ethics: An Introduction to Moral Philosophy* (2d ed.; New York: McGraw-Hill, 1991).

8. Ibid., 16–22.

9. Gottfried Wilhelm Leibniz, *Leibniz Selections*, ed. P. P. Weiner (New York: Scribner's, 1951), 534.

10. John Donne, *Devotions upon Emergent Occasions: Together with Death's Duel, Meditation 17* (Ann Arbor: University of Michigan Press, 1959).

5. Morality and Other Social Institutions

1. Hillary Rodham Clinton, *It Takes a Village* (New York: Simon & Schuster, 1996).

2. Merle Travis, "Smoke, Smoke, Smoke That Cigarette," written for Tex Williams, recorded by Capitol Records, 1947.

3. A fascinating study of the history of America's battle with tobacco in the late nineteenth and early twentieth centuries can be found in Cassandra Tate, *Cigarette Wars: The Triumph of "The Little White Slaver"* (New York: Oxford University Press, 1999).

6. Questions about the "Non-moral"

1. William Frankena, *Ethics,* 2d ed. (Englewood Cliffs, N.J.: Prentice-Hall, 1973), 7.

2. Ibid., 10f.

7. Degrees of Moral Density

1. William Frankena, *Ethics,* 2d ed. (Englewood Cliffs, N.J.: Prentice-Hall, 1973), 11. Frankena's example is "You ought to buy a new suit."

2. Oliver O'Donovan, *Resurrection and Moral Order: An Outline for Evangelical Ethics*, 2d ed. (Grand Rapids: Eerdmans, 1994), 199.

9. Morality and Ethics

1. Carol Gilligan, *In a Different Voice: Psychological Theory and Women's Development* (Cambridge: Harvard University Press, 1993).

2. Sidney Callahan, *In Good Conscience: Reason and Emotion in Moral Decision Making* (San Francisco: Harper, 1991).

3. R. M. Hare, *The Language of Morals,* reprint (Oxford: Clarendon, 1991).

11. Deontology and Universal Moral Obligations

1. Alasdair MacIntyre, *A Short History of Ethics* (New York: Macmillan, 1966), 190.

2. Immanuel Kant, *Fundamental Principles of the Metaphysic of Morals,* trans. T. K. Abbott (Buffalo: Prometheus, 1987).

3. Sisela Bok, *Lying* (New York: Pantheon, 1978).

4. John Rawls, *A Theory of Justice* (Cambridge: Belknap, 1971).

5. For a wide discussion of various understandings of justice, see Karen Lebacqz, *Six Theories of Justice* (Minneapolis: Augsburg, 1986), and Alasdair MacIntyre, *Whose Justice? Which Rationality?* (Notre Dame: University of Notre Dame Press, 1988).

6. Thomas Nagel, *The Last Word* (New York: Oxford University Press, 1997), 5.

7. Paul Ramsey, *The Patient as Person* (New Haven: Yale University Press, 1970).

8. Paul Ramsey, *Ethics at the Edges of Life* (New Haven: Yale University Press, 1978).

9. Paul Ramsey, *The Just War* (Lanham, Md.: University Press of America, 1983).

10. W. D. Ross, *The Right and the Good* (Oxford: Clarendon, 1930).

12. Situationism and Appropriate Actions

1. Joseph Fletcher, *Situation Ethics* (Philadelphia: Westminster, 1966).

2. Harvey Cox, ed., *The Situation Ethics Debate* (Philadelphia: Westminster, 1968).

3. John A. T. Robinson, *Honest to God* (London: SCM, 1963).

4. John A. T. Robinson, *Christian Morals Today* (Philadelphia: Westminster, 1964), 20.

5. Bob Dylan, *The Times They Are A'Changin'*, Warner Bros., 1964; renewed 1991, Special Music Rider.

6. Harvey Cox, *The Secular City* (New York: Pantheon, 1978).

7. G. Ernest Wright and Reginald Fuller, *The Book of the Acts of God* (Garden City: Doubleday, 1957).

8. Dorothy L. Sayers, *The Man Born to be King: A Play-cycle on the Life of our Lord and Saviour Jesus Christ* (New York: Harper and Brothers, 1943), 5.

9. Cox, *The Secular City*, 125f.

10. Daniel Callahan, ed., *The Secular City Debate* (New York: Macmillan, 1966).

11. David L. Edwards, ed., *The Honest to God Debate* (London: SCM, 1963).

12. Ernest Hemingway, *A Farewell to Arms* (New York: Macmillan, 1929), 184f.

13. An interesting study is found in Norman N. Greene, *Jean-Paul Sartre: The Existentialist Ethic* (Ann Arbor: University of Michigan Press, 1963).

14. Simone de Beauvoir, *The Ethics of Ambiguity*, trans. B. Frechtman (New York: Philosophical Library, 1948), 158.

15. Thomas C. Oden, *Radical Obedience: The Ethics of Rudolf Bultmann* (Philadelphia: Westminster, 1964), 38.

16. Jean-Paul Sartre, *Essays in Existentialism* (Secaucus: Citadel, 1965) from Tom L. Beauchamp, *Philosophical Ethics* (New York: McGraw-Hill, 1982), 325–28.

17. Joseph Sittler, *The Structure of Christian Ethics* (Louisville: Westminster John Knox, 1998), 82f.

18. Paul Lehmann, *Ethics in a Christian Context* (London: SCM, 1963).

19. For a splendid treatment of the work of Paul Lehmann, see Nancy J. Duff, *Humanization and the Politics of God: The Koinonia Ethics of Paul Lehmann* (Grand Rapids: Eerdmans, 1992).

20. H. Richard Niebuhr, *The Responsible Self* (New York: Harper & Row, 1963).

13. Teleology and the Common Good

1. William Frankena, *Ethics* (Englewood Cliffs, N.J.: Prentice Hall, 1973), 14f.

2. Tom L. Beauchamp, *Philosophical Ethics: An Introduction to Moral Philosophy*, 2d ed. (New York: McGraw-Hill, 1991).

3. Robin Gill, *A Textbook of Christian Ethics* (Edinburgh: T. and T. Clark, 1995).

4. In the second edition, Beauchamp adds a fourth method, which he calls communitarian theory. In my opinion, communitarian theory is best treated as a form of character ethics.

5. For a specific and clear statement of this, see Bultmann's review of Oscar Cullmann's *Christ and Time*. Rudolf Bultmann, "History of Salvation and History," *Existence and Faith,* trans. Schubert M. Ogden (New York: Meridian, 1960), 226–40.

6. Frankena, *Ethics,* 14.

7. A splendid introduction is *dialog,* vol. 34, no. 4 (Fall, 1995) with the theme "The Common Good."

8. Some useful resources are Jeremy Bentham, *An Introduction to the Principles of Morals and Legislation* (Oxford: Clarendon, 1823); John Stuart Mill, *Utilitarianism,* ed. G. Sher (Indianapolis: Hackett, 1979); Anthony Quinton, *Utilitarian Ethics* (New York: Macmillan, 1973); J. J. C. Smart and Bernard Williams, *Utilitarianism: For and Against* (Cambridge: Cambridge University Press, 1973).

9. *Commonweal,* 475 Riverside Drive, New York, NY 10115, ed. Margaret O'Brien Steinfels.

10. Robert N. Bellah, et al., *Habits of the Heart* (Berkeley: University of California Press, 1985).

11. Robert N. Bellah, et al., *The Good Society* (New York: Knopf, 1991).

14. Character Ethics and the Virtues

1. Lee H. Yearley, "Recent Work on Virtue," *Religious Studies Review,* vol. 16, no. 1 (January, 1990), 1.

2. Dietrich Bonhoeffer, *Ethics,* ed. E. Bethge (New York: Macmillan, 1965), 64f.

3. Martin Luther, "The Freedom of a Christian," *Three Treatises* (Philadelphia: Fortress, 1960).

4. Aristotle, *The Nicomachean Ethics,* trans. David Ross (Oxford: Oxford University Press, 1991).

5. Ibid., 14.

6. Lewis B. Smedes, *A Pretty Good Person* (San Francisco: Harper, 1991), 174.

7. Martin Luther, *Treatise on Good Works, Luther's Works*, vol. 4 (Philadelphia: Fortress, 1966).

8. Gilbert Meilaender, "Living with Aristotle and Luther," *Forum Letter,* vol. 14, no. 2 (March 1, 1985), 7.

9. Gilbert Meilaender, *The Theory and Practice of Virtue* (Notre Dame: University of Notre Dame Press, 1984).

10. Gilbert Meilaender, *Friendship: A Study in Theological Ethics* (Notre Dame: University of Notre Dame Press, 1981).

11. Alasdair MacIntyre, *After Virtue* (Notre Dame: University of Notre Dame Press, 1981).

12. Jean Porter, *The Recovery of Virtue: The Relevance of Aquinas for Christian Ethics* (Louisville: Westminster/John Knox, 1990).

13. Stephen L. Carter, *Integrity* (New York: Basic, 1996), and *Civility: Manners, Morals, and the Etiquette of Democracy* (New York: Basic, 1998).

14. Sara Lawrence-Lightfoot, *Respect: An Exploration* (Reading, Mass.: Perseus, 1999).

15. William J. Bennett, ed., *The Book of Virtues: A Treasury of Great Moral Stories* (New York: Simon & Schuster, 1993).

16. William J. Bennett, ed., *The Moral Compass: Stories for a Life's Journey* (New York: Simon & Schuster, 1995).

17. William J. Bennett, ed., *The Children's Book of Virtues* (New York: Simon & Schuster, 1995).

18. Richard George Adams, *Watership Down* (New York: Scribner, 1996).

19. Stanley Hauerwas and William H. Willimon, *Resident Aliens: Life in the Christian Colony* (Nashville: Abingdon, 1990).

20. H. Richard Niebuhr, *Christ and Culture* (New York: Harper, 1951).

15. Making Methodological Commitments

1. See Albert R. Jonsen and Stephen Toulmin, *The Abuse of Casuistry: A History of Moral Reasoning* (Berkeley: University of California Press, 1988).

2. Marcia W. Baron, Philip Pettit, and Michael Slote, *Three Methods of Ethics: A Debate* (Malden, Mass.: Blackwell, 1997).

16. Considering Consequentialism

1. Samuel Sheffler, ed., *Consequentialism and Its Critics* (Oxford: Oxford University Press, 1988).

2. J. J. C. Smart and Bernard Williams, *Utilitarianism: For and Against* (Cambridge: Cambridge University Press, 1987). See also J. J. C. Smart, *Ethics, Persuasion and Truth* (London: Routledge & Kegan Paul, 1984).

3. Paul Ramsey, "The Justice of Nuclear Deterrence," in Robin Gill, *A Textbook of Christian Ethics* (Edinburgh: T. & T. Clark, 1985), 377.

4. Joseph Fletcher, *Situation Ethics* (Philadelphia: Westminster, 1964), 120.

17. Consequentialism and Practical Wisdom

1. Edward O. Wilson, *Consilience: The Unity of Knowledge* (New York: Vintage, 1999).

2. Immanuel Kant, *Fundamental Principles of the Metaphysic of Morals,* trans. T. K. Abbott (Buffalo: Prometheus, 1987), 11.

3. George Edward Moore, *Principia Ethica* (Cambridge: Cambridge University Press, 1962). See also Chapter 2, "Interlude on the Naturalistic Fallacy" in J. J. C. Smart, *Ethics, Persuasion and Truth.* For further discussion on this topic, see my article, "Doing What Comes Naturally: Christian Ethics and the Is/Ought Question," *dialog* 25, no. 3 (summer 1986): 186–92.

4. W. D. Hudson, *The Is/Ought Question* (New York: St. Martin's, 1969).

5. Quoted in Robin Gill, *A Textbook of Christian Ethics*, 2d ed. (Edinburgh: T. and T. Clark, 1995), 271.

6. Immanuel Kant, *Religion within the Limits of Reason Alone*, trans. T. M. Greene and H. H. Hudson (LaSalle: Open Court, 1960).

7. Bernard Williams, *Ethics and the Limits of Philosophy* (Cambridge: Harvard University Press, 1985).

8. Daniel Callahan, *Setting Limits: Medical Goals in an Aging Society* (Washington, D.C.: Georgetown University Press, 1995).

9. Dietrich Bonhoeffer, *Ethics,* ed. E. Bethge (New York: Macmillan, 1965), 235.

18. A Unified Field Theory of Ethics

1. Stephen W. Hawking, *A Brief History of Time* (New York: Bantam, 1988), 175.

2. See Michael Ignatieff, "On Isaiah Berlin (1909–1997)," *The New York Review of Books* (December 18, 1997): 10. He says, "He seemed like the quintessential fox, but now that his journey is completed, it is possible to see that he was a hedgehog all along. The unity to his work grew from a sustained concentration on what he took to be the Enlightenment's central flaw: its belief that the truth was one. . . ."

19. Calculating Probable Outcomes

1. Among the many helpful treatments of the use of the Bible in Christian Ethics is the study by Allen Verhey, *The Great Reversal: Ethics and the New Testament* (Grand Rapids: Eerdmans, 1984).

2. *The Didache or the Teaching of the Twelve Apostles,* trans. J. A. Kleist (Westminster, Md.: Newman, 1948), 16.

3. Martin Luther, *Luther's Works,* vol. 21, ed. J. Pelikan (St. Louis: Concordia, 1956), 115–18.

4. Herman Wouk, *Inside, Outside* (New York: Avon, 1985), 381.

5. Sharon D. Welch, *A Feminist Ethic of Risk* (Minneapolis: Fortress, 1990).

20. Jesus Christ and the Future of God's Creation

1. See J. N. D. Kelly, *Early Christian Creeds* (New York: Longman, 1972), and *Early Christian Doctrines* (London: A. and C. Black, 1977).

2. It should be noted that the phrase "and the Son" is included in the confession by the churches in the West but omitted by the Orthodox churches of the East. The debate about these words (the *filioque* phrase) goes back to the sixth century.

3. There is legitimate debate among scholars concerning the Pauline authorship of Colossians. My own judgment is that the weight of the evidence is on the side of Paul as author.

4. A few centuries later, it was essentially this same gnostic understanding of who Jesus is that was spread widely in the early church by Arius. Athanasius called the Council of Nicea in 325, and finally in 381 at Constantinople, the Nicene Creed was completed. Every phrase was directed at the Arian view, which was very similar to the problem in Colossae to which Paul writes.

5. The material was later published under the title "The Cosmic Christ," *Religion and Society* 8, no. 4 (1961): 38–42.

22. Afterword—Believing and Behaving

1. Joseph Sittler, *The Structure of Christian Ethics* (Louisville: Westminster John Knox, 1998).

2. C. H. Dodd, *The Apostolic Preaching and Its Developments: Three Lectures with an Appendix on Eschatology and History* (New York: Harper, 1950).

3. C. H. Dodd, *Gospel and Law: The Relation of Faith and Ethics in Early Christianity* (New York: Columbia University Press, 1951).

4. Karl Barth, "Gospel and Law," *Community, State, and Church: Three Essays* (Garden City, N.Y.: Doubleday, 1960), 71–100.

5. Karl Barth, *The Humanity of God* (Richmond: John Knox, 1960).

6. Karl Barth, *Christ and Adam: Man and Humanity in Romans 5,* trans. T. A. Smail (New York: Harper, 1957).

7. Karl Barth, *The Faith of the Church: A Commentary on the Apostles' Creed according to Calvin's Catechism,* ed. J.-L. Leuba, trans. G. Vahanian (New York: Meridian, 1958), 113f.

8. H. Richard Niebuhr, *Christ and Culture* (New York: Harper Collins, 1986).

9. For example, Hauerwas and Willimon say, "We have come to believe that few books have been a greater hindrance to an accurate assessment of our situation than *Christ and Culture.*" Stanley Hauerwas and William H. Willimon, *Resident Aliens: Life in the Christian Colony* (Nashville: Abingdon, 1990), 40.

10. James M. Gustafson, *Christ and the Moral Life* (New York: Harper & Row, 1968).

11. Ibid., 240.

23. Afterword—Moral Directives and Action Directives

1. Dietrich Bonhoeffer, *Ethics,* ed. E. Bethge, trans. N. H. Smith (New York: Macmillan, 1965), 196–207.

2. See James H. Burtness, *Shaping the Future: The Ethics of Dietrich Bonhoeffer* (Philadelphia: Fortress, 1985).

3. Dietrich Bonhoeffer, *Ethics,* 188.

4. For important discussions about the connection between Christian faith and environmental concerns, see Larry L. Rasmussen, *Earth Community, Earth Ethics* (Maryknoll: Orbis, 1996), and Daniel C. Maguire and Larry L. Rasmussen, *Ethics for a Small Planet: New Horizons on Population, Consumption, and Ecology* (Albany: State University of New York Press, 1998).

5. Thomas Aquinas, "Natural Law" in Robin Gill, *A Textbook of Christian Ethics,* 2d ed. (Edinburgh: T. & T. Clark, 1995), 82.

24. Afterword—Civil Conversation about Serious Disagreements

1. Robert Darnton, "Free Spirit," *The New York Review of Books* (June 26, 1997), 9–11.

2. These suggestions can be found with additional material in my article "When Christians Disagree" in *The Lutheran* (August 9, 1989), 12–14.

Index

A-P